Ex Libris

Mary Ann Williams

THE STORY OF AMERICA IN PICTURES

THE STORY OF
AMERICA
IN PICTURES

ARRANGED BY ALAN C. COLLINS

INTRODUCTION BY CLAUDE G. BOWERS

THE LITERARY GUILD · NEW YORK

AUTHOR'S NOTE

★

ALTHOUGH an effort has been made to secure pictures for this
book which would portray faithfully each event, the compiler
realizes that many famous historical paintings were conceived
without full and accurate knowledge of the facts, and that some
of them were even done with the intent to romanticize the
event or person in question. Therefore, it cannot be said that
every picture herein is absolutely accurate, although the
"spirit" of the scene may be carefully portrayed.

In reading THE STORY OF AMERICA IN PICTURES the Outline,
which appears in the front part of the volume, should be used.
In it the period of our history has been marked off into the ten
"eras" into which it rather naturally divides itself. In order to
avoid confusion, it has been thought wise to group the events
taking place within the time-period of each of these ten major
divisions in subdivisions. In doing this, the character of the
event in question has been the determining classifying factor.
Although making for historical unity, such a plan has made impossible a strictly chronological plan throughout.

Furthermore, it has been thought best to leave the flow of
the pictures uninterrupted, and to confine dividing marks between divisions and subdivisions to the Outline. Reference to
this will simplify the use of the book and show why, within the
scheme, the sequence of events is not chronological.

The compiler of this book wishes to express his appreciation
of the assistance Mr. D. Jay Culver of New York City has been
to him in collecting many of the illustrations, especially for
the years prior to 1900.

August 19, 1935.

OUTLINE

★

INTRODUCTION

★

THE MOST FASCINATING HISTORY is pictorial, even though the pictures are in words. In his *French Revolution*, Carlyle has given us a magnificent gallery of paintings, and his book consequently is immortal.

The story of the past can be made deadly dull unless so told as to make the visualization of the scene possible. Because so many histories do not call forth pictures, history has been given a bad name among the masses to whom history is important.

Woodrow Wilson was convinced that the highest art in the historian is in the painting of the contemporary scene in the very atmosphere of the times. He believed in pictures. A distinguished friend and associate of the War President has collected all the moving pictures covering his career, and, by running them in their order of precedence, has preserved for the historians of posterity a more vivid and human record than can possibly be put in words.

It is easy to forget the details of what one reads; one never forgets the details of what one sees. Many years ago a few friends met in the bar of the old St. Charles hotel in New Orleans. Included in the party was Sergeant S. Prentiss, the most brilliant orator America has produced. The conversation turned to a lecture on art, being given that night by a famous critic to raise money for an art museum. Prentiss and one of the party preceded the others to the theater. As the others approached the meeting, a little later, they were amazed to hear roars of applause. The critic was not an orator. As they entered the theater they found the explanation—Prentiss was speaking. Summoned to the stage without notice, he had plunged with all his eloquence into an oration on the masterpieces of art, which, in mangled form, is happily preserved today. Not an artist, not a student of art, he had nevertheless been able on a moment's notice to speak on art with a brilliancy that few, if any, of his contemporaries could have approached. And the reason was that during a vacation a little before he had amused himself by turning the pages of a great portfolio of the artistic masterpieces of the world. He put the pictures he had seen in words. He felt the pictures as no reading of a text-book could have made him feel them.

By the same token the ideal way to study history is to journey to the scenes associated with mighty events after having read the story of what had occurred there. The layman may read and reread the descriptions of the battle of Gettysburg and remain in utter ignorance of the movements of the troops; but no man can visit the battlefield with its monuments, today, without being able to call before him the dramatic scenes in the clashing of the blue and gray. That which the eye sees is most deeply imprinted on the mind.

In this volume the compiler has sought, at great pains, to collect the pictures that most vividly tell the story of the United States from the beginning almost to the present hour. It is a panoramic history that is rich in inspiration. It serves a patriotic purpose in bringing before us each step of our development, and impressing upon us, as words can scarcely do, the Homeric achievements of our people. No written chronicle of England from the Boer War to the present can make the emotional appeal to be found in "Cavalcade." In the picture one can recapture the very emotions of the times.

And no nation lends itself more perfectly to the pictorial history than our own. Our progress has been all drama, and much can be told in pictures. Few nations have been more colorful in their story. Within the space of a few centuries we have seen a vast continent redeemed from the wilderness, and our people marching with giant and gallant stride to their place in the sun. This has been due to the youthful vigor and romantic daring of our race. Our story is a picturesque drama with innumerable scenes. The drama is here presented in pictures.

Here we have the discoverers giving a new continent to civilization, battling against savage natives and more savage nature, penetrating the wilderness, pushing through primeval forests, floating down unknown streams, planting blockhouses as the outposts of a new day. That is drama at its highest.

And then we see the pioneers settling in the wilderness, living in log huts, felling the forests, draining the swamps, bridging the streams, building the highways, cultivating the fields, erecting schoolhouses and churches—and that is drama too.

And then the pictorial drama of the Revolution—Patrick Henry in fiery action, Jefferson in the preparation of the Declaration, Washington and his ragged continentals, and in the camp that dismal winter at Valley Forge. And then that dramatic, colorful scene at Yorktown. The whole drama of the Revolution can be told in pictures.

The flag unfurled—and the flag moves on toward the far Pacific. Louisiana's destiny is joined with ours, an event as rich in color as any we have ever known. And, in the meanwhile, the pioneers of the tribe of Daniel Boone are building their cabins in the woods and guarding them with their long rifles.

And then the genius of Jefferson launches our first scientific expedition on the waters of the far West when Lewis and Clark, with a few audacious and hardy hunters and fighters, tramp the virgin wilderness or float in canoes on the swift and dangerous streams, and break a path for civilization through the forests and across the mountains to the western sea, battling against disease and hunger. What a picture!

The War of 1812? It can be recorded in three pictures—Washington in flames, Perry on Lake Erie, and Andrew Jackson behind the cotton bales in New Orleans.

The flag moves on, fluttering among the wild passes of Mexico as our brave soldiers charge their bloody way to victory—and California is ours!

And soon the discovery of gold in the new possession, and that can be told in pictures—the wild rush of rough enterprising men in search of fortune, the opening of mines, the army with picks, the wild scenes in the camps.

And then, the opening of the western lands to settlement, and the picturesque procession of the covered wagons, men, women, children, and dogs, over trackless miles—laughter and tragedy, smiles and tears; and finally the garden spot of America blossoms. What drama! What a picture!

Then comes the War between the States, and, for the first time on a large scale, photography takes up the work of the historian, and through the illustrated weeklies the folks at home can visualize the immortal struggle—the clash of armies, the scenes about the camps, the swinging march of soldiers along the dusty highways—Gettysburg, Missionary Ridge, the battles of the Wilderness. These pictures, happily preserved, tell the tale of superhuman courage and sacrifice.

And other wars—Dewey at Manila Bay, the battle of Santiago Harbor, the passionate charges on San Juan Hill; and then the World War, when, rising to unprecedented heights of idealism, two million youths in a crusading spirit sailed across the sea to perform miracles of building and fighting and to end the dreadful struggle of humanity. But

> *"Peace hath higher tests of manhood*
> *Than battle ever knew."*

xiii

And the story of the United States confined to battles fought with sword and gun is a story scarcely told. The peculiar splendor of our national development with such unprecedented rapidity lies in our victories over material forces—in the creation of our industrial life.

This, too, can be told in pictures. The building of the railroads is all romantic drama, with heroes and villains—tremendous in the dreams of the builders, in the labor of the workers, in the audacity of the conceivers—a story as picturesque and thrilling as any in all the tide of time. And this drama of the building is preserved in pictures.

Not always admirable were the methods of the amazing figures who pioneered our industrial and financial life. There was, too often, the savage, selfish spirit of the ruthless individualist, who, convinced of the ultimate gain for all, brushed all ethics aside to press on with brutal force to the achievement. Happily the story of this industrial growth and financial development, as told in pictures, presents only the more inspiring side. There are few exceptions—the marching of Coxey's army, the picture of "Black Friday."

The whole of our history cannot be told in pictures, but through them we get the highlights; and when they cover the whole of our story from the discovery to the present we may in the course of an evening visualize and catch the spirit of the nation's onward march. Nothing could be more useful or desirable now when the cynic and the scoffer are so blatant in the land. "New occasions teach new duties," and changes inevitably must come to meet changed conditions. But each succeeding generation has rendered heroic service, stumbling and blundering as all human creatures must, but always moving forward. Here we have presented to the eye a remarkable collection of pictures through which our inspiring history marches in parade. They bring us nearer to the past, on which the present rests; they inspire us with a greater reverence for the dead generations that have fought and wrought magnificently for us, and they revive within us something of the old dreams and ideals.

CLAUDE G. BOWERS

American Embassy,
Madrid,
July 24, 1935

INDIANS OF THE FOREST

There is no present unanimity of opinion as to the origin of the people found in North America by the early explorers. Scholars agree that at one time northwestern America and northeastern Asia belonged to the same cultural area, but whether the Indians came from Asia or the Asiatics from America is not established. For purposes of rough classification the Indians here when Columbus arrived divide into three groups, Indians of the forest, Indians of the plains, and Indians of the west and southwest.

INDIANS OF THE PLAINS

The various tribes of the forest differed but they had much in common because their mode of life was the same. The men hunted, mostly deer, and made war. Some fishing was done and the women made attempts at agriculture. They traveled on foot and in canoe, but the forest was their home, supplying them with virtually all their worldly wants. Vastly different were the many tribes of the interior who inhabited the great plains swarming with buffalo. They likewise lived by hunting, but agriculture played a somewhat more important part in their lives. It was not until they caught and tamed the progeny of the horses that had escaped from the Spanish conquerors that they secured mounts for hunting and warfare.

INDIANS OF THE WEST

The tribes of the southwest were mostly Pueblos. They lived in permanent houses, often many stories high, in which each room was the home of a family. They had developed agriculture to a high degree, possessed some domesticated animals, and had mastered the science of irrigation. There were tribes of a different sort in California, while to the south dwelt the Aztecs, and beyond them was the vanished culture of the Mayas. Despite his savagery, the Indian was possessed of much dignity and simple wisdom, bred in him by the vast areas of virgin land which were his home and his heritage.

LEIF ERICSSON DISCOVERS VINLAND

Many scholars claim that the hardy Viking, Leif Ericsson, discovered America. Son of Eric the Red who colonized Greenland, Leif, in about the year 1000, landed on a coast which he called Vinland, for some of his men had seen wild grapes growing. This was prob- ably either Nova Scotia or the New England of later times. Such was the shadowy prologue. It was to be almost five hundred years before the real drama of American history began.

18

COLUMBUS AND QUEEN ISABELLA

As the 15th century drew to a close, the world was ready for the real discovery of America. Some people were saying that the world was round and had asserted that it might be possible to reach the riches of the east by sailing west. It was assumed that the same ocean washed the coasts of China and Europe. The increasing restlessness found its "man of the hour", in Christopher Columbus. He had unshakeable faith in an idea and was willing to risk his life for it. He said he would reach the Orient by sailing into the Atlantic. For ten years he haunted the courts of Europe seeking a financial backer. At length the necessary money was borrowed on security offered by the Queen of Spain. That she offered her jewels for the purpose may be only a legend.

FROM THE PAINTING BY VACSLAV VON BROZIK.   COURTESY ART EDUCATION PRESS, INC., NEW YORK.

19

THE VOYAGE OF COLUMBUS

Orders were issued to outfit Columbus with three tiny ships and, after great difficulties in securing crews, he set sail from Palos on August 3, 1492. A stop was made at the Canary Island's. Columbus kept two log books, one for himself and one to show his doubting crew. In early October the men began to grumble openly; some suggested throwing Columbus overboard. But the faith of the commander prevailed.

THE LANDING

On the evening of October 11th lights were seen, and the next day Columbus stepped ashore in the new world on a small island in the Bahamas, probably that which is now known as Watling's. The natives told him, by signs, of a country to the south. Toward it he sailed and found Cuba, but he was convinced that he had found the mainland of India. He then skirted Haiti, left half his men to plant a colony, and returned to Europe.

FROM THE PAINTING BY JOHN VANDERLYN.

THE CABOTS LEAVING LABRADOR

England's early claims to America had little to do with any exploration by her own citizens. John Cabot, born in Genoa and a citizen of Venice, induced Henry VII to outfit an expedition. In 1497 and 1498 Cabot, probably accompanied by his son Sebastian, explored the coast from Newfoundland to South Carolina. But England forgot the work of the Cabots until a century later, when she was only too anxious to recall their discoveries.

VASCO DA GAMA IN KALIKUT

A Portuguese navigator succeeded where Columbus had failed. In 1497 da Gama set out to discover the mysterious empire to the east. Heading into the south Atlantic, and then turning east, he sighted the African coast near the Cape of Good Hope, in the discovery of which he had however been anticipated by Diaz. Rounding that "land's end" he continued east and so, at last, was found the water route to India. He claimed the country and returned home in triumph. The picture was made in 1747.

23

PRINTING VESPUCCI'S BOOK

Amerigo Vespucci survives in history because from him derive the names of two continents. He accompanied an expedition to South America in 1499. Years later there was published his account of the trip, in which he told of the wondrous sights he had seen, giving the impression that he was in command of the vessel and that its voyage antedated the third made by Columbus. Waldseemüller, a geographer, having Vespucci's account, and not that of Columbus, accepted the former's story and in 1507 called the new continent America, after the author's first name.

THE FOUNTAIN OF YOUTH

To the Spaniards in the West Indies the natives brought tales of a great land in which there was a spring having the power to confer perpetual youth. In 1513 Ponce de Leon set out to find the magic waters, and discovered the mainland near St. Augustine. He named the country Florida, sailed down the east coast of the peninsula, and part way up the west, and returned through the previously unknown Bahama Channel, a protected strip of water which was later to be the haunt of pirates.

CLAIMING THE PACIFIC

Balboa fled from his home in San Domingo pursued by debt, and seized the rule of a struggling colony in Darien. From there he journeyed overland to prove the truth of Indian reports of a vast ocean to the west. Coming to a ridge, he made his companions remain be-hind and, reaching the summit, first discovered the mighty Pacific. When he had made the long journey to the shore he plunged into the water, claiming on September 29, 1513, all the ocean in the name of the King of Spain.

MAGELLAN SAILS AROUND THE WORLD

Magellan, an expatriated Portuguese, whose expedition was the first to circle the earth, sailed from Spain in 1519. He discovered the tortuous passage around the tip of South America and eventually came out on the waters first seen by Balboa. He named the ocean Pacific because of its gentle breezes. Reaching the Philippines after suffering great hardships he died. Sebastian del Cano continued the voyage, eventually bringing to Spain the great news that at last the east had been reached by sailing west.

CORTEZ CAPTURES MEXICO CITY

Hernando Cortez left Cuba in 1519 to conquer Mexico. Reaching the mainland his boats became worm-eaten and sank. (Some say he burned them
purposely.) At any rate, with his escape cut off, it was a question of win or
perish. Fighting his way to the capital he captured Montezuma, butchered
the natives, and helped himself to a vast wealth of gold and silver. His
brilliant campaigns made many at home jealous and he was forced to
return to Spain. He made another voyage, and on returning from it was
received coldly by the king. Perhaps there was truth in his bitter taunt
that he had given his sovereign more provinces than his ancestors had be-
queathed him cities.

28

DISCOVERY OF THE MISSISSIPPI

One of the victims of the reputed wealth of "the Floridas" was Hernando de Soto who had had his appetite for gold whetted by the fortune he had acquired accompanying Pizarro to Peru. He sold part of his property, outfitted an expedition, and landed in Florida in 1539. The next four years he spent marching through the Southern states, ever seeking for gold, until in 1541 he came to the Mississippi. He crossed the river and explored the present states of Arkansas and Louisiana. As the party was returning in 1542 along the Mississippi De Soto died and his men buried him in the waters of the great river he had discovered. Although he had dissipated his fortune in a vain quest for riches, he accomplished a far worthier result in opening a vast territory for those who followed.

FROM THE PAINTING BY POWELL.

29

FROM THE PAINTING BY FREDERIC REMINGTON IN "OLD SANTA FE TRAIL" BY HENRY INMAN, 1898, PUBLISHED BY CRANE & CO., TOPEKA, KANSAS.

CORONADO IN THE SOUTHWEST

Led on by tales of seven cities to the north, each one as rich as the great one in Mexico found by Cortez, Francisco de Coronado with a large expedition turned northward from New Spain in 1540. He explored our southwest. He found Indians living in pueblos and saw buffalo, but no gold, and returned home. In thirty years the Spaniards, seeking wealth, had opened up Mexico and the Southern and Southwestern United States for the real work of colonization.

RALEIGH: QUEEN ELIZABETH COMMISSIONS HIM TO SAIL FOR AMERICA

Sir Walter Raleigh was the first man to visualize America as a place in which Englishmen might find homes, not wealth. He attempted to have Virginia colonized in 1584, again in 1585, and for a third time in 1587. This last expedition was led by John White, an incompetent who chose the poor soil of Roanoke on which to settle. He saw the colony launched and then hurried back to England for supplies and new settlers.

COURTESY FRICK ART REFERENCE LIBRARY.

31

CROATOA

THE LOST COLONY

When White left, the remaining colonists promised that if they moved away they would leave behind them the name of their destination. In 1591, when he returned, the word "Croatoan," the name of a tribe of Indians, was found on a tree. The colonists had vanished. Years later the settlers learned they had gone to the Indians. If any escaped massacre they were doubtless absorbed into one of the Indian tribes, and a tradition to this effect has continued throughout the centuries. So ended the attempt to settle a colony in America.

SETTLEMENT IN 1607.

In 1606 a better organized attempt was made to settle Virginia by the London Company. Advantage was taken of the mistakes at Roanoke, and a landing was made at Jamestown in 1607. The colony's sponsors in England decreed that it be ruled by a board of seven men, and the sealed document embodying this decree was opened just before landing. But it was an impossible type of government, and Edward Wingfield, one of the seven, soon was chosen president. The picture shows the arrival of a ship from England, bringing supplies and new settlers to the struggling colony.

SETTLERS IN JAMESTOWN

The new colony did not prosper. All profits from the venture were to go to the sponsors, the London Company, and so the powerful impetus of private gain was absent. Moreover, some settlers had little desire for work and were inclined to sit by while indentured serv- ants performed the manual labor. Disease, idleness, and incompetence very nearly extinguished in its first years this fourth attempt by Englishmen to settle America.

34

THE LEGEND OF JOHN SMITH AND POCAHONTAS

By his energy and resourcefulness John Smith soon displaced Wingfield and became the acknowledged leader in Jamestown. On one of his expeditions to the Indians to barter for food Smith was captured. According to a tale told by Smith many years later, he was saved from death only when Pocahontas, daughter of the powerful chief Powhatan, begged for his life. Smith advanced the colony but when he sailed for England things sank back again, and the winter of 1609–1610 was known as the "starving time."

MARRIAGE OF POCAHONTAS

Although some doubt has been cast on the story of Pocahontas and John Smith, it is certain that this attractive Indian maiden was the first convert of her people to Christianity. She married John Rolfe, one of the early settlers. Many families still prominent in Virginia trace their ancestry to this marriage, including that of the Bollings, one member of which was the second wife of President Woodrow Wilson.

ATTACK BY THE INDIANS

It was Sir Thomas Dale, a harsh tyrant, who eventually set Jamestown on a permanent foundation. He forced the idle to work and ruthlessly killed those who shirked. In 1622 the Indians, seeking to protect their land, slaughtered four hundred settlers; and in 1644 three hundred more. In later years a system of great estates, so characteristic of the South, was to come into being, based on slave labor, the growing of tobacco, and still later, the growing of cotton.

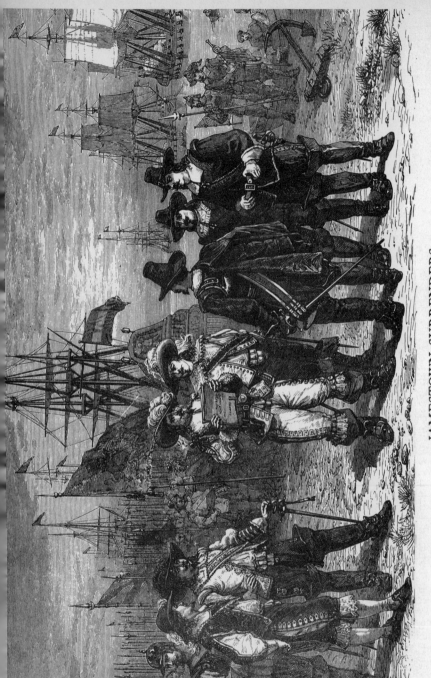

JAMESTOWN SURRENDERS

The colony grew rapidly and by 1650 held more than 15,000 inhabitants. The long and prosperous tenure of Sir William Berkeley, although a proud and arrogant governor, had much to do with the changed conditions. One of his wisest decisions was to surrender peaceably in March, 1652, to a fleet sent over by Parliament. By this he not only saved bloodshed but also many of Virginia's charter rights.

BACON'S REBELLION: ASKING AID OF BERKELEY

In 1675 the colony was again menaced by Indian raids and the settlers on the borders came to Berkeley asking aid. He refused it and soon the people began to raise troops under Nathaniel Bacon. To Berkeley, this was treason. Bacon turned against him. He seized and burned Jamestown. On Bacon's death from fever the revolution collapsed, but it had shown how Virginians felt toward arbitrary emissaries of the king, and it was an omen of 1776.

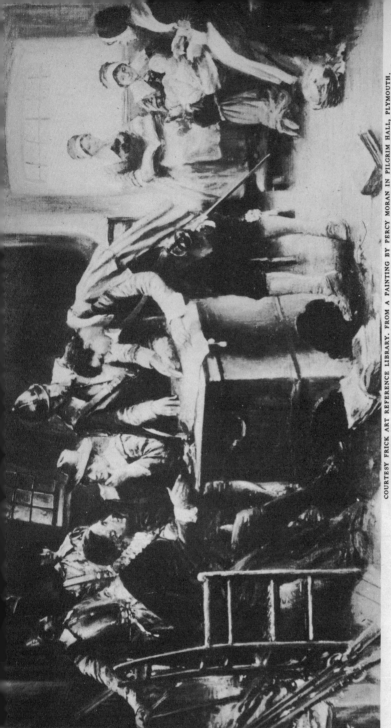

SIGNING THE MAYFLOWER COMPACT

The Pilgrims, separatists from the Church of England, first went to Holland in their search for a place where they might worship according to their beliefs, but after ten years in that country, finding that their children were growing up to be more Dutch than English and not having prospered financially, they determined to settle in America. One hundred and two of them sailed in the famous *Mayflower* in 1620. Before landing they signed the famous Mayflower Compact which looked towards the establishment of a democratic form of government for the colony.

THE LANDING OF THE PILGRIMS

The *Mayflower's* objective was Virginia but, sighting Cape Cod, the Pilgrims chose, after weeks of exploration, the present site of Plymouth for their home. On December 26th they came ashore. They were almost as poorly equipped to fight the wilderness as were the Virginians.

Their religion, an absolute faith in a literal reading of the Bible, together with their plain speech, plain clothes, and modest bearing, were, however, not unsuited to the trials ahead.

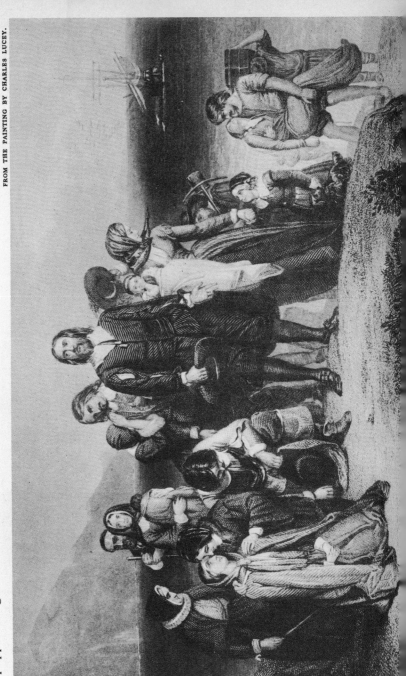

FROM THE PAINTING BY CHARLES LUCEY.

DEPARTURE OF THE "MAYFLOWER"

When the *Mayflower* sailed away the last tie with home was cut. The Massachusetts winter had set in and food was scarce. By spring, fourteen of the eighteen wives who had sailed in the ship died. When a good crop was eventually harvested a Thanksgiving Day was set aside to commemorate it. Governor Bradford's good sense in dealing with the Indians and in abolishing communal labor had much to do with saving the colony.

PILGRIMS GOING TO CHURCH

The colony at Plymouth, after the first few years, took on a semblance of permanence. Education was begun and, of course, attendance at church was the accepted thing. The Pilgrims were, however, far less militant in their religion than the Puritans who, in 1629 and 1630, settled the larger colony of Massachusetts Bay. They arrived in force at Salem, then Boston, and finally settled seven other towns. They were recruited from the business men of England and brought the instinct for trade with them to the new world.

43

SLAUGHTER OF THE PEQUOTS

As the colonies expanded trouble with the Indians was inevitable. In 1637, stirred by a common enemy, the whites joined against the Pequots in an inter-colonial war managed by the Massachusetts colony and the Connecticut towns. John Mason and John Underhill were the leaders. The Indians were cornered. Of some four hundred men, women, and children, only four escaped alive. The Pequot tribe was extinguished by this and a subsequent bloody slaughter which, although cruel, gained peace for the colony for many years.

44

JOHN ALDEN AND PRISCILLA

Miles Standish's gruff character as a soldier has lent credence to Longfellow's story of his courtship of the pretty Priscilla Mullins. It is a popular legend that the bashful Standish sent John Alden to court Priscilla for him and that she, knowing Alden's heart was not in his mission, suggested that he speak for himself. Alden did marry her, however. He lived to be the only surviving member of the original *Mayflower* company.

45

STOPPING A FARMHOUSE FROLIC

"Puritanism" in American life and letters has become a symbol of restraint. It placed a curb on the boisterous expression of natural good spirits, and was for many years a restraining influence on the social life of New England. Of great influence were the divines, John Cotton, and Cotton and Increase Mather. After their decline there was a lull until the fiery Jonathan Edwards stirred for the last time the dying embers of religious and semi-religious frenzy.

ENDING THE REVELS AT MERRYMOUNT

It must be remembered that the Puritans came to America not to set up a colony for free worship but to set up a home where they might worship as they chose. A corollary of this was their readiness to impose their ideas on others; and against Thomas Morton, a carefree adventurer, they discovered a dual reason for taking action. He was their rival in the profitable fur trade and soon felt the force of their righteous arms. One day they appeared at his settlement, tore down his gay maypole, put an end to his revels, and banished him to England.

ROGER WILLIAMS ARRIVES IN RHODE ISLAND

Roger Williams was another to fall afoul of the Massachusetts authorities. He was banished because, among other things, he maintained that to acquire land legally, the colonists must buy it from the Indians. Escaping from Massachusetts, he founded Providence in 1636, the first colony in which religious toleration became a reality. He made friends with the savages, and through this friendship, rendered valuable service to his late oppressors during their war with the Pequots.

FROM THE PAINTING BY ALONZO CHAPPEL.

48

ENDICOTT REMOVES THE CROSS

One of the most forceful personalities among the Puritans was John Endicott, rash, bigoted, and brave. He it was who first purchased from the Plymouth Company several miles of Massachusetts coast, extending westward to the Pacific, and settled Salem. He was both a leader in the Pequot War, and one of the chief persecutors of the Quakers. One of his exploits was the cutting of the cross from the king's ensign, even this symbolism being contrary to his scruples.

WHIPPING QUAKERS

The Puritans could not stem the rising tide of liberal thought in the colony, but they tried. First Mrs. Anne Hutchinson, a lady of fine birth, was banished for expressing her religious convictions, and the subsequent slaughter of her entire family by the Indians was considered a judgment of God. Next they turned on the Quakers, even putting some of them to death. Massachusetts was unique in the length to which it went in these persecutions.

THE SALEM WITCH TRIALS: A GIRL BEWITCHED

The darkest blots on early New England history are the witchcraft killings in Salem of 1691 and 1692. In all about thirty people, mostly friendless old men and women, were put to death, one by the horrible method of crushing with heavy weights. The evidence which was presented in court by those who claimed they had been bewitched made a mockery of English justice. The craze finally collapsed as suddenly as it had started.

HARVARD COLLEGE

Education was a primary concern of the New Englanders. In 1649 a law was passed requiring every town of more than fifty families to support a school. Meanwhile, in 1636 Harvard College, the only center of higher learning for half a century, had been founded. This view of early Harvard was engraved by Paul Revere who, thrifty soul, cut off during the Revolution the missing half of the plate that he might use the copper to engrave bank notes.

DUTCH AND ENGLISH QUARRELS IN CONNECTICUT

It was natural that with a colony started in Massachusetts, the English should spread to the rest of what they called New England. The Dutch were in what is now Connecticut before them, however, having planted a settlement at the present site of Hartford in or previous to 1633. The two were soon in conflict and quarrels were not uncommon. Temporary peace was established in 1650. The government established to the south differed in one important respect from that of Massachusetts in that there was no religious test for citizenship.

53

54

CATCHING, DRESSING. AND DRYING THE COD, FROM KEITH'S. VIRGINIA, 1738.

EARLY INDUSTRY

In the century and a half from the actual colonization of the new world to
the outbreak of the Revolution, America passed through the first stage of
her industrial development. The first settler and his wife had, of necessity,
to make most of what they needed with their own hands. Gradually, as the
social system crystallized and money began to circulate, there grew up a
place for the skilled artisan. By the middle of the 18th century a high degree of commercial self-sufficiency had been attained. Although labor-
saving devices (machinery) were beginning to make an appearance in
England by 1790, it was not until after the War of 1812 that Americans
made the first steps from artisan labor to the factory system.

WEYMOUTH ON THE KENNEBEC

There is no certainty as to who first discovered the coast of Maine. In 1605, however, George Weymouth was sent to "North Virginia" to maintain English claims of prior possession. He journeyed up the Kennebec River, the shores of which entranced him with their virgin beauty. Unfortunately for later settlers, and for the victims, he kidnaped several Indians whom he took back to England.

56

LANDING OF HENRY HUDSON

At about the same time that Virginia was being settled, the Dutch began moving into the area dominated by the Hudson River. They sent Hudson in 1608 to discover a northwest passage to China. This was much the same objective that led on the great company of early explorers, a century and more before. Hudson failed to find the passage and turning south at last entered New York Bay. In 1609 he sailed up the mighty river, named after him, to what is now Albany, and a small boat was sent even further. Hudson's discoveries proved that the river did not lead to China, that there was no isthmus in North America as there was at Panama, and led directly to Dutch colonization.

FIRST SETTLEMENT ON MANHATTAN

Hudson's explorations revealed the value of the river valley. The first houses on Manhattan sprang up around a trading post on the southern tip, established by the Dutch. In 1621 New Netherland was put under the newly chartered Dutch West India Company which sent out directors to govern it. In 1623 or 1624 about thirty Walloon families arrived, but all but eight of the men in the company continued up the river to settle Fort Orange, now Albany.

THE PURCHASE OF MANHATTAN

In 1626 Peter Minuit negotiated the famous purchase of Manhattan Island for cloth, beads, and other trinkets to a total value of about $25. The Dutch later made an attempt to transplant the patroon system to the region dominated by the upper Hudson, but feudalism in any form was unsuited to the wilderness. Although the number of colonists increased slowly, the town gradually assumed a prosperous, even a wealthy, air. The comfortable life of the traders of this era shaped its social and economic structure for many years after Dutch rule disappeared.

PEACE WITH THE INDIANS

When Peter Minuit retired troublous times came to the colony. Governor van Twiller met opposition to Dutch expansion in Connecticut and along the Delaware. His successor, William Kieft, arriving in 1638, found himself faced with the necessity of arousing a sluggish population to fight the Indians. To conduct the war he im- ported John Underhill, one of the leaders in the Pequot War slaughters, from New England, and peace eventually was made in 1646. Kieft finally gave way willingly to Peter Stuyvesant, last and greatest of the Dutch governors.

FALL OF NEW AMSTERDAM: STUYVESANT MARCHES OUT

Stuyvesant was stubborn, brave, hard-hearted, and possessed of a violent temper, but withal a good governor. He did more to improve the physical condition of the city than all his predecessors. The English, who had never given up claim to all the Atlantic coast, decided in 1664 it was time to eliminate the Dutch. A fleet appeared in the harbor and Stuyvesant, pegging up and down on his wooden leg, vowed he would fight. But the city was defenseless, the people were opposed to him, and he was finally led forcibly by them from the ramparts without a gun being fired. The Atlantic seacoast from Maine to Florida was in English hands.

CARTERET LANDING IN NEW JERSEY

With the fall of New Amsterdam, New Jersey was granted to the Duke of York and that same year he conveyed it to Lord John Berkeley and Sir George Carteret. Berkeley sold his interest to two Quakers. Later, one of these two disposed of his share to three Quakers, one of whom was William Penn. Later still, the three acquired the share of the other Quaker. The quinpartite deed of 1676 gave Carteret East Jersey and the Quakers West Jersey. Carteret's land was put on the auction block in 1682 and Penn and eleven associates bought it in for £3400. The twelve were later doubled in number and in 1701-2 all the proprietors surrendered their rights of jurisdiction.

PENN'S TREATY

In settlement of a debt owed to his father, Charles II gave William Penn a grant of land in the new world. In 1682 the young Quaker, fired with the idea of governmental and religious freedom, sailed up the quiet waters of the Delaware to take possession of his grant. The name Pennsylvania is the Latinized form of Penn's Woods. Almost Penn's first act was to make a treaty with the Indians, and his next was to establish for his colony a liberal form of self-government.

PENN'S COLONISTS ON THE DELAWARE

At the confluence of the Schuylkill and the Delaware River, Penn established Philadelphia, the town of "Brotherly Love," laying out an architectural plan of rectangular divisions bounded by broad straight roads or streets—a design which was one of the earliest city planning projects that later served as a model for many other cities throughout the world. All men who pro-fessed faith in Christ were invited to come there. English, Welsh, and Germans flocked to the new colony, and so rapid was the growth of Penn's "green country town" that it soon surpassed the older settlements of Boston and New York, becoming the foremost commercial center of colonial America.

64

FRANKLIN IN PHILADELPHIA

Franklin and Philadelphia. It was the "happy marriage" of our early history. The story of his arrival in the city as a poor boy with a loaf of bread under his arm is a true American legend. The secret of his success was his rare common sense and his ability to make others see a plain fact, plainly arrived at. He was a printer and publisher, an inventor, a scientist, a philosopher, a public-spirited citizen, and a statesman. Before he died he was hailed as the "wise man" of the new nation.

THE STATE HOUSE

Although the French and Indian wars upset the borders, life in and around Philadelphia continued peaceful and prosperous up to the Revolution, in comparison with the disturbances in the other colonies. Despite quarrels with Penn's heirs, relations with the proprietors in England were fairly amicable. The city's landmark was the State House (later Independence Hall), built between 1731 and 1751. In the additions to it, built in 1791, sat the Supreme Court and the Congress.

66

DE VRIES VISITS HIS RUINED COLONY

The Dutch colony established by David De Vries in Delaware was destroyed by the Indians in 1632. De Vries wrote that he found there only "the skulls and bones of our people." Other Dutch settlements followed and a conflict with the Swedes, who had also settled on Delaware Bay, ensued. Peter Stuyvesant conquered the settlements of New Sweden but in 1664, when New Netherland fell, Delaware also became English. Although the colony had an independent legislature it was governed by the chief executive of Pennsylvania, under the Duke of York's grant to Penn, down to 1776. Maryland, by reason of Baltimore's grant, did not release claim to all of Delaware until 1767, when the present dividing line between the two states was laid down.

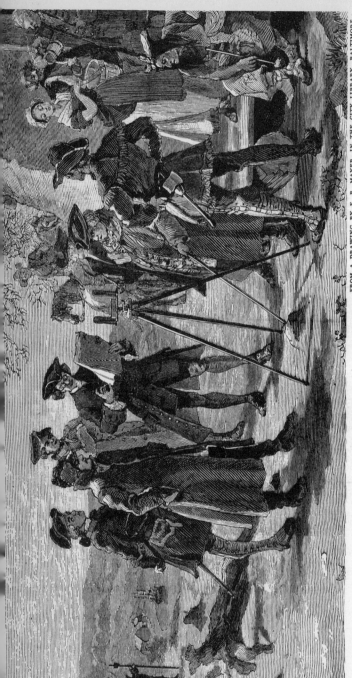

LAYING OUT BALTIMORE

George Calvert, the first Lord Baltimore, obtained from James I a grant of lands near the James River where he thought he and other Catholics might find a haven of peace. The actual grant was issued to the son, Cecilius Calvert, in June, 1632. The "Charter of Maryland," containing the patents to the Lords Baltimore then and in future, was noteworthy in its guarantees of freedom of government, even freedom from taxation by the crown, and freedom of religion. Cecilius delegated command of the expedition to his younger brother, Leonard Calvert. He was accompanied by two Jesuit priests, Father Andrew White and Father John Altham, and in all about 300 emigrants. They sailed on November 22, 1633, in two ships, the *Ark* and the *Dove*, and landed in Maryland (named after the Queen) on March 25, 1634, the "day of the Annunciation of the Most Holy Virgin Mary"; they planted a great cross of wood and knelt around it while the litany was read.

68

FROM B. J. LOSSING'S "OUR COUNTRY."

THE CAROLINAS: SETTLERS

Although some colonists had filtered southward from Virginia the settlement of the region between that colony and Florida was placed by the king in the hands of eight of his friends, who became the Proprietors. Two regions developed, bearing the names North Carolina and South Carolina. The latter, with important West India connections, the investment of greater capital, and the cultivation of rice and indigo on plantations worked by Negro slaves, became the richer and more aristocratic. North Carolina was relatively poor, and democratic. Both passed safely through the dangerous Indian wars. After much disorder, both colonies became royal colonies when the Proprietors sold their rights to the crown.

OGLETHORPE'S FIRST INTERVIEW WITH THE INDIANS

James Oglethorpe, moved by the wretched condition of the prisoners in English debtors' prisons, secured permission to start a colony in Georgia in 1733. There was also in view the idea of making the colony a line of frontier defence against the Spaniards to the south. This was the last unsettled land between Maine and Florida. Oglethorpe made peace with the Indians, forbade the introduction of slaves and rum, and limited the land holdings of each settler. These restrictions did not attract new colonists and prosperity was slow in coming until they were relaxed in 1749. Spain never had given up her claim to the southern coast and much of the time up to 1748, when the dispute was settled, was consumed with beating back the ambitious Spaniards.

SLAUGHTER OF THE FLORIDA HUGUENOTS

Although the Spaniards were the first to explore Florida they were slow to settle it. In 1564 De Laudonnière, the Huguenot leader, established at Fort Caroline a French settlement. The Spaniards realized that if their returning treasure ships were to be safe the land could not remain in enemy hands. Pedro Menendez was sent to rout the French. He not only routed them but butchered those who surrendered.

71

LAYING OUT ST. AUGUSTINE

Leaving a garrison at Fort Caroline, Menendez founded St. Augustine in 1565, the first permanent settlement in America. It has been said, though without satisfactory proof, that the French were not slow in dealing with their enemies. Dominique de Gourgues, suddenly appearing at Fort Caroline, killed all who resisted and hanged the prisoners. If this actually happened, it was an act of useless cruelty, for the French made no further attempts to expand there and Florida remained Spanish until it was purchased by the United States in 1819.

72

BUCCANEERS CAPTURING A SHIP

So long as Spain controlled the sea routes her treasure ships returning from the New World were relatively safe; but when the Spanish Armada was defeated, the pirates, English, Dutch, and French, began to intercept the stream of returning treasure. These picturesque murderers and highwaymen of the sea came from all stations in life. They flourished in the 16th century and on one occasion a pirate fleet is said to have captured at Vera Cruz booty worth $30,000,000.

73

VERRAZANO AT NEWPORT

Giovanni da Verrazano, an Italian, was the first to establish any French claim to the new world. He was sent out by Francis I in 1524 to find a route to China by way of a western waterway. Touching at about Cape Fear on the present coast of North Carolina, he sailed north. He discovered the Hudson River, and may have found the present Narragansett Bay, Newport harbor, and even the Gulf of St. Lawrence.

CARTIER AT HOCHELAGA

The voyages of Jacques Cartier were the real bases of French claims to Canada. In 1534 he set out to find the passage to China that had evaded so many others. That year and the next he explored the St. Lawrence as far as Montreal, where he visited the Indian village of Hochelaga. Aside from one abortive effort at Quebec in 1541 no serious effort at colonization was made until the coming of Champlain.

CHAMPLAIN SURRENDERS QUEBEC

Samuel de Champlain established Quebec in 1608, appreciating that that site was the key to the St. Lawrence River valley. He explored much of the country and made frequent trips to France to advance Quebec's interests. He was forced to surrender his beloved city to the English and the Iroquois in 1629 but when Canada was restored to French hands he came back to his post. His wife, whom he had married when she was but twelve, became a nun on his death in 1635.

CHAMPLAIN FIGHTING FOR THE INDIANS

One unwitting act of Champlain's lost the French all chance of expansion southward. He accompanied the Algonquins in a war party against the Iroquois in 1609. Two being shot by him, the Iroquois fled and the Algonquins roared with laughter at seeing their enemies so easily routed, but the French were henceforth to find the powerful Iroquois unalterably opposed to them in New York. On this trip Champlain discovered the lake named after him and in 1615 became the first white man to see the Great Lakes.

THE JESUIT BRÉBEUF

The arrival of the Jesuits gave impetus to expansion in New France.
These fine men came to convert the Indians and to advance the fur trade
for their country. They were successful with the Algonquins and the
Hurons, but the Iroquois were implacable. Many of these French missionaries were killed, including Brébeuf, after excruciating torture. Following
the Jesuits came the Ursulines, a teaching order, and the *Hospitalières*
who were nurses. The Récollets were present before the Jesuits, but their
ten years of missionary work convinced them that a richer, better organized
group was needed to carry on.

78

RADISSON AND GROSEILLIERS IN THE WEST

Champlain was followed by Nicolet who explored westward to Lake Michigan. At one point in his journey, Nicolet, thinking he neared China, dressed himself in ceremonial robes. A quarter-century later Radisson and Groseilliers followed him and explored Lake Superior. Later, transferring their allegiance for a while to England, they were instrumental in establishing the Hudson's Bay Company's lucrative fur trade. The age of expansion, in which France claimed by right of original exploration all territory from Hudson's Bay to the Gulf and west to the Rockies, had begun.

JOLIET AND MARQUETTE ON THE MISSISSIPPI

That France failed to win all America except the coastal fringe of English colonies was, in the end, due to two factors. Too few settlers came to her settlements, and French sea power, the only method of communication with New France, was surpassed by the British. Two noted explorers of the Golden Age of exploration were Father Marquette, a Jesuit, and Joliet, a trader. They pushed beyond Lake Erie, descended the Mississippi to Arkansas in 1673, and then turned back fearing that the news of their great discoveries would perish with them at the hands of the Spaniards.

LA SALLE CLAIMS THE MISSISSIPPI

La Salle completed Marquette's work. Although undoubtedly a visionary he was the first to grasp the magnificent idea of a great French empire in the interior of America. In the time of the great Frontenac, the finest governor New France ever enjoyed, La Salle headed for the Mississippi which he appreciated was the key to his imaginary empire. He reached the Gulf in 1682 and, being assured by the Indians that he was the first white man to explore the river, claimed its valley for the king of France.

MURDER OF LA SALLE

The next year La Salle was in France. His plan was to settle Louisiana and an expedition was fitted out for him, but his ships, missing the delta, took him far to the west of the Mississippi. He spent the last months of 1685 in Texas vainly searching for his beloved river. He finally gave up and in 1687 turned north. His men were grumbling at the rigorous manner in which he ruled them, and finally one of the company killed him by shooting him in the back.

FRONTENAC: THE ATTACK ON QUEBEC IN 1690

Count Frontenac, a vigorous soldier, was France's opening gun in the battle for North America. Louis XIV sent him back to Canada as governor in 1689, for trouble with the English (King William's War) was just beginning. He carried out a series of bloody raids in New York, New Hampshire, and Maine. An expedition sent against him at Quebec in 1690 was a disastrous failure. Nevertheless the war dragged on for seven years. Neither side gained appreciably in this first trial of arms. It was the prelude to a struggle which was to continue for three quarters of a century.

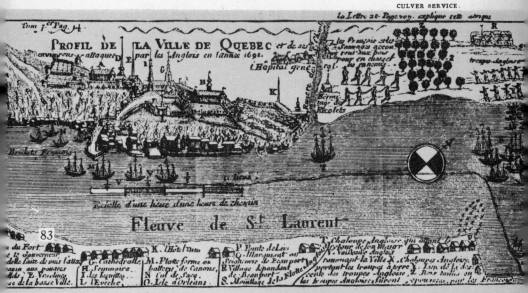

PLAN OF ATTACK ON QUEBEC, 1690.[1]

1 Fac-simile of an engraved plan in La Hontan's *New Voyages*, London, 1703, vol. i. p. 160. It was re-engraved for the French edition of 1705.

BIENVILLE'S ARMY ON THE RIVER

La Salle's work was completed by d'Iberville and Bienville. The former planted in 1699 the first trading post in Mississippi and the latter founded New Orleans in 1718. Both places had enormous possibilities which were never realized. Although Cadillac was to found Detroit in 1701 and La Verendrye's sons possibly to see the Rockies in 1743, the great age of French exploration was over. The wars with the English and the Indians in the north put an end to the dream of a French empire on the Mississippi.

PORTOLÁ DISCOVERS THE GOLDEN GATE

The period which witnessed the decline of Spanish power in Europe saw the steady growth of her influence in southwestern America. Explorers and missionaries pushed their way into Lower California and then into California. An expedition under Don Gaspar de Portolá left San Diego in July, 1769, and a few months later emerged from the forest to see stretched below the great harbor of San Francisco Bay and the rock pillars of the Golden Gate.

PERILS OF OUR FOREFATHERS

Two basic conflicts were inherent in our colonial life, one between the settlers and the Indians (wars similar to that with the Pequots ravaged virtually all the colonies), and another between the English and the French. Both conflicts continued up to the eve of the Revolution. The French held Canada, including the St. Lawrence, and the Mississippi. They wanted the Hudson. The English wanted to push west. Where outposts of the two touched, only warfare could settle the issue.

86

KING PHILIP'S WAR: DEATH OF PHILIP

Philip, a Wampanoag, began the war that bears his name in 1675. The struggle was marked by ruthless slaughter on both sides, with complete annihilation of the enemy the one objective. Eventually the superior organization of the whites turned the balance. Although King Philip was killed in 1676, the struggle dragged on. During the fight the whites suffered serious losses of men, and great destruction of their crops and homes, but as a result the Indian menace in southern New England was removed.

ANDROS A PRISONER

Philip's war was no sooner over than another danger appeared. Charles II
and James I intended to revoke the charter rights of the colonies and make
them royal provinces. Connecticut, alarmed, hid her charter in an oak
tree but even she submitted when Edmund Andros arrived in 1688 as the
royal governor. His harsh rule, carried on in defiance of charter rights, was
a short one, for when James was overthrown in England, the people rose
and put Andros in jail.

PEPPERELL AT THE SIEGE OF LOUISBOURG:
KING GEORGE'S WAR

With King William's War, 1690–1697, began the serious conflicts with the
French. It was followed by Queen Anne's War, 1701–1713, and King
George's War, 1744–1748. In the first neither side gained, in the second the
English won Acadia (Nova Scotia), Newfoundland, and Hudson's Bay.
In the third William Pepperell captured the powerful fortress of Louisbourg,
only to lose it under the unwise terms of the Treaty of Aix-la-Chapelle.
These three wars were the prelude to the last act of the drama in which the
curtain was to be forever rung down on the epic of French empire in the
New World.

BRADDOCK'S DEFEAT

The last act of the drama of the struggle for North America, the French and Indian War, was begun in 1754 with each side prepared to fight to a decision. As a first move, the English sent General Braddock in 1755 against Fort Duquesne. Near there his expedition was ambushed. His Virginia troops fought as did the Indians, from behind trees, but Braddock forced his regulars into solid files where they were excellent marks for the concealed enemy. He himself was wounded and about half his force was killed. George Washington, already winning fame as a brilliant commander, played a brave part in the retreat.

READING THE DECREE EXPELLING THE ACADIANS

The English now decided to make solid their hold on Nova Scotia, and the expulsion of the Acadians was agreed on. It is doubtful whether these farming people were a real menace but the English thought they were and, assembling them in their village churches, read to them the decree of expulsion. They were forced on ships and scattered heartlessly throughout the colonies. Longfellow has told a romantic story of this unnecessary brutality in *Evangeline*.

91

MONTCALM STOPPING THE MASSACRE AT FORT WILLIAM HENRY

The year 1757 brought a serious English disaster. Fort William Henry had remained in English hands until that year, when its garrison marched out before Montcalm, the last great man in New France. Then the tragedy occurred. Montcalm could not restrain the blood lust of his Indian allies who set on the defenseless men. The French general risked his life to halt the slaughter, but at least fifty were tomahawked before his troops put an end to it.

92

WASHINGTON AT FORT DUQUESNE

The pace now quickened, for Pitt was in the saddle in England determined to force affairs, at long last, to a conclusion. A terrific bombardment forced the heroic defenders of Louisbourg to surrender to Lord Jeffrey Amherst in 1758. In New York, despite the catastrophe at Ticonderoga, Fort Frontenac was taken, and the same year Fort Duquesne was abandoned by the French to an expedition headed by John Forbes, in which Washington had a subordinate command. It was the beginning of the end, for both wings of the French dominions had begun to crumble, one on the Atlantic, the other on the Great Lakes.

FROM THE PAINTING BY I. R. CHAPIN.

DEATH OF WOLFE ON THE PLAINS OF ABRAHAM

At last the way was clear for the real objective of all this warfare—Quebec. Against it by sea came the greatest war fleet to cross the Atlantic up to 1917. Against it by land came eight thousand troops under General Wolfe. Montcalm, deserted by the government in Paris and harried by intrigue and corruption within the walls of Quebec, prepared to resist. Wolfe determined to make the decisive attack by land and on September 13, 1759, he fought the brilliantly conceived Battle of the Plains of Abraham. Both he and Montcalm fell, but Quebec was in British hands at last. Unparalleled scenes of celebration took place in London and the colonies. The next year Montreal fell and France laid down her arms in the new world forever. The dream was over.

PONTIAC UNITING THE TRIBES IN CONSPIRACY

Because the French were defeated, all was not yet safe for the ever-expanding English. Pontiac, as able an Indian as has ever lived, united the jealous tribes for one final effort, in 1763. Had he lived a hundred years earlier he might have succeeded. He led his followers to many victories but the end was never in doubt. Pontiac died at the hands of one of his own race who, for a barrel of rum, struck him down from behind. Pontiac's war for the ever-expanding English. Pontiac, as able an showed London that the menace of the frontier remained. Ten thousand troops were accordingly kept in the colonies and it was planned to support them in part by the proceeds from the Stamp Tax, resistance to which was one of the links in the chain of events leading to the Revolution.

BURNING THE STAMPED PAPER

Several factors helped bring about the Revolution but one of the most important was the question of taxation. Parliament claimed the right to tax the colonies, while they resisted on the ground that they had no voice in the matter. In 1765 was passed, however, the Stamp Act. Instant and violent were the protests. The tax could not be, and never was, enforced. It was repealed in 1766 and by its very repeal British prestige suffered a severe blow.

THE "BOSTON MASSACRE"

No less irritating than taxes was the presence of 10,000 British troops in New England. To the claim that they were necessary for defense, the colonists asked why they had not been sent when protection was needed against the French and Indians. Whatever other reasons there may have been, the troops were in Boston partly to keep the hot-headed New Englanders in leash. Bloodshed was avoided for a time but in 1770, stung to fury by the taunts of the people, and finally one soldier being struck, a shot was fired. Before the trouble ended, five lay dead. The fat was in the fire. The average man understood the language spoken by bullets.

FROM THE PAINTING BY ALONZO CHAPPEL.

THE BOSTON TEA PARTY

After an effort at further taxation in 1767, designed to recognize a distinction between external and internal taxes, all these duties were repealed in 1770 except the tax on tea. Three years later Parliament passed another law which permitted the East India Company to export part of the tea stored in its warehouses free from all English duties, but subject to the tax levied for American ports. Part of this tea was about to be landed in Boston when on the night of December 16th a crowd of men dressed as Indians boarded a British ship and dumped its cargo of tea into the harbor. No taxed tea was wanted in Boston.

FIRST CONTINENTAL CONGRESS: DELEGATES LEAVING CARPENTERS' HALL

The rising tide of opposition to British rule finally brought about that which had never before been possible—sustained unity of action among the colonies. Hitherto, local jealousies and conflicting interests had kept them apart. Now, the rights of all were menaced. Virginia sent out the call for delegates to attend a Continental Congress. Philadelphia was chosen as a meeting-place, and on September 5, 1774, representatives of all but Georgia began sessions in Carpenters' Hall. The ablest leaders in America attended.

PATRICK HENRY IN THE FIRST CONTINENTAL CONGRESS

A radical party, not yet daring to broach independence, and a conservative element, for allegiance to the king, soon materialized. Despite this difference, resolves were passed in which the colonies claimed the right to legislate for their own affairs, and the rights inherent in personal and political liberty. Finally, a compact was made not to import from or export to Great Britain, after certain dates. With this, the Congress, which had served chiefly to unite the Whigs, adjourned.

PAUL REVERE'S RIDE

In the spring of 1775 Gage determined to break the gathering storm and dispatched troops to Concord, eighteen miles from Boston, to seize a supply of the colonists' military goods. Paul Revere, warned of this decision by a prearranged signal, a lantern hung in the North Church, rode through the night warning the farmers and the Minute Men, a body of militia formed but a few weeks before, of the coming of the British. He reached Lexington in time but was captured before he came to Concord.

FROM "HARPER'S WEEKLY," JUNE 29, 1867.

BATTLE OF LEXINGTON

FROM A PAINTING BY ALONZO CHAPPEL.

In addition to the stores at Concord, the object of the British was the arrest of the radicals Samuel Adams and John Hancock. When the column arrived at Lexington shortly after dawn on April 19th, about a hundred militia opposed them. There was a shot, then a volley, and the colonials fled, leaving eight dead. The British lost not a man. The military significance of Lexington was infinitesimal, its political significance was, and still is, stupendous.

RETREAT FROM CONCORD

After Lexington the British pushed on to Concord and, covering the bridge, made a gesture at destroying the colonial stores. Those at the bridge were soon attacked by an overwhelming number of militia, the whole body being forced to retreat to Boston. The shot "heard around the world" had been fired and the Revolution had begun. During the retreat the red coats of the British made easy marks for the Americans, sharpshooting from farmhouse windows and from behind fences and trees. The finest British troops had been surrounded, ambushed, and outflanked. The wonder is that they escaped complete capture.

BATTLE OF BUNKER HILL

On June 16th the Americans fortified Bunker and Breed's hills overlooking Boston. Gage's besieged position in the city was now more than ever insecure. His troops attacked the next day but were twice driven back by the defenders who withheld their fire "until you see the whites of their eyes." Such was the practise of good frontier marksmen. On the third charge the Americans, their ammunition exhausted, retired. In the end the British carried the hill but the moral effect of the strong American defense, against able and well-trained troops, was great.

FROM THE PAINTING BY ALONZO CHAPPEL.

104

WASHINGTON TAKES COMMAND

War was now on in earnest and the army needed a general. Congress appointed George Washington, a gentleman from Virginia and a soldier trained in the Indian wars, to that position, and what had been a New England army became a Continental one. From the moment that he took command in Cambridge Washington never had a full quota of troops and was continually hampered by desertion and discontent. It was his patience, his firm hand, and the confidence and respect he inspired in men universally, as much as his ability as a commander, which brought the war to a successful conclusion six years later.

FROM A PAINTING BY ALONZO CHAPPEL.

CAPTURE OF FORT TICONDEROGA

Now came one of those incidents which make the history of the Revolution so colorful. Ethan Allen of Vermont, on his own initiative, raised the "Green Mountain Boys," and proceeded against Ticonderoga. He surprised the garrison, and took the fort "in the name of God and the Continental Congress." The supply of guns, ammunition, and heavy cannon which he captured were desperately needed at Cambridge, especially the cannon which later played a part in taking Boston.

106

DEATH OF MONTGOMERY IN THE EXPEDITION AGAINST CANADA

Now came Benedict Arnold's daring march to Canada which although in the end a failure, came astonishingly near success. Its real objective was the winning of the Canadians to the American cause. Washington gave his full approval. Suffering incredible hardships, Arnold marched his men north through the approaching winter of 1775. Another column under Montgomery joined him after taking Montreal. Their joint attack on Quebec was a failure, Montgomery was killed, and Arnold retreated to Crown Point, contesting every foot of the way.

HOWE EVACUATING BOSTON

Meanwhile the British remained besieged in Boston. In the spring of 1776 Washington determined to bring the matter to a head. In a surprise move, he took Dorchester Heights. After that the city was at the mercy of the cannon captured at Ticonderoga. Lord Howe embarked his eleven thousand soldiers, together with the Loyalist inhabitants, and sailed for Halifax. He left behind him a prodigious amount of supplies and military stores which Washington greatly needed.

FROM THE PICTURE BY M. A. WAGEMAN.

108

STIRLING'S RETREAT AT THE BATTLE OF LONG ISLAND

After Boston, Washington marched to New York. The British plan was to capture the city, proceed up the Hudson, and so split the colonies in two. Washington, unwisely, decided to contest the issue on the heights of Brooklyn. There poor generalship accomplished his defeat on August 27, 1776. With his army in immediate danger of capture, Washington now brought about one of the most brilliant retreats in military history—the secret transfer of his entire army across the East River to Manhattan. He himself escaped with the last of the troops.

FROM A PAINTING BY ALONZO CHAPPEL.

EXECUTION OF NATHAN HALE

Nathan Hale's farewell words, "I regret that I have but one life to lose for my country," are part of our tradition. He was a young man. When the British occupied Manhattan, Washington was in continual need of knowledge about Howe's plans. Hale volunteered to secure this information. He disguised himself as a Dutch school-teacher and entered the city, but the British captured him and after a trial before Howe he was hanged as a spy.

BATTLE OF HARLEM HEIGHTS

Washington's parting shot after abandoning New York was the Battle of Harlem Heights on September 16th which he won. There followed in rapid succession a defeat at White Plains, and the loss of Forts Washington and Lee. By these victories Howe gained control of the lower Hudson and had he pushed on he might have ended the war in late 1776, but he allowed Washington to escape and retreat across New Jersey to the south side of the Delaware at Trenton.

FROM "HARPER'S WEEKLY," SEPTEMBER 30, 1876.

FROM THE "NEW YORK MIRROR," SEPTEMBER 24, 1842.

WASHINGTON CROSSES THE DELAWARE

Frederick the Great once said that Washington's successes between December 24, 1776, and January 4, 1777, were "the most brilliant" in military history. Moving quickly, he pushed his way through the ice-clogged Delaware, marched to Trenton through the sleety night, and early in the morning of December 26th captured the surprised town. Still moving fast he was back across the river before he could be caught, only to recross it again on the last day of the year. Then he struck, again with lightning speed.

BATTLE OF PRINCETON

Circling the enemy flank he fell on a large column at Princeton, routing it in the early morning of January 3rd. These victories stayed the desertions that were decimating his ranks and brought new recruits to him in the spring. After adroit maneuvering in New Jersey in the summer of 1777, Howe sailed for the Delaware but ended by entering Chesapeake Bay. Washington followed cautiously and south of Philadelphia on the Brandywine Creek on September 11, he was defeated in a battle which he should have won. Howe then invested Philadelphia.

FROM THE PAINTING BY TRUMBULL.

113

MURDER OF JANE McCRAE

The Saratoga campaign of 1777, a sequel to Arnold's stubborn retreat from Canada, was a complete American victory. By this Burgoyne was prevented from joining hands with Howe in New York and so cutting off Washington's retreat through New Jersey. Schuyler, Lincoln, and Gates commanded the campaign, but Arnold played a large part in bringing about success. One act of some Indians, supposed to be allied with Burgoyne, helped to bring the militia flocking to the American side. This was the abduction and murder of Jane McCrae. Hearing of it, the population rose in arms on all sides.

ARNOLD WOUNDED AT SARATOGA

Burgoyne advanced slowly, his forces suffering successive defeats at Bennington, in the Mohawk Valley, and twice at Freeman's Farm. Indecisive action accomplished his defeat. He turned back on Saratoga but by now the Americans had him surrounded. On October 17, 1777, he surrendered his entire army. Success in this campaign was due more to the subordinates, Stark, Lincoln, Morgan, and Kosciuszko than to the commander, Gates. The American victory was the turning point of the Revolution. It is counted among the decisive battles of the world.

115

BATTLE OF GERMANTOWN

Washington was determined to surprise the British in Philadelphia. On a foggy morning in early October four columns marched on the city by separate roads. In Germantown the battle seemed won, but the British barricaded Judge Chew's mansion and there resisted Washington's main column stubbornly. The retreating troops rallied. General Greene's men, usually reliable, lost their way in the fog and then one of his subordinates, being intoxicated, caused the soldiers under him to fire into Wayne's troops. Washington's brilliant plan was a failure and he retreated to Valley Forge.

FROM THE PAINTING BY ALONZO CHAPPEL.

116

DE KALB INTRODUCING LAFAYETTE TO SILAS DEANE

When news of Saratoga arrived in Paris the task of securing a French alliance, assigned to Silas Deane and Benjamin Franklin, became easier. A promise of men, money, and ships was quickly made. Equally as important to the American cause were the volunteers, Lafayette, de Kalb, Pulaski and Kosciuszko, the Poles, and Von Steuben, a Prussian. Inspired by our struggle for independence they all rendered valuable service, especially the youthful Lafayette who became Washington's lifelong friend and confidant.

WASHINGTON'S TROOPS AT VALLEY FORGE

The winter at Valley Forge was Washington's low point. His rival, Gates, had received credit for Saratoga while he himself had done little but retreat and suffer defeats since Princeton. Congress now became critical of his military tactics. In addition, it failed to supply his men with food and clothing, many of whom fell sick and died in the rude snow-bound huts above the Schuylkill. Meanwhile, the British danced, wined, and slept peacefully in the comfortable city of Philadelphia. The bright spots in the winter were the budding confidence in Lafayette and the services of Von Steuben, the drill master. When spring came to the rolling Pennsylvania hills he had made well-disciplined soldiers out of the raw recruits.

118

BATTLE OF MONMOUTH

The British now left Philadelphia, Washington trailing them cautiously to Monmouth, New Jersey, where the two armies met on June 28, 1778. It was a blazing hot day. Charles Lee, in command of the attack, lost Washington the great opportunity for which he had been waiting, and for which Von Steuben, Lafayette, and Greene had labored in the dark days at Valley Forge—the capture of the British army or a large part of it. Lee retreated almost without having attacked. He was later dismissed from the army for his conduct. Monmouth was the last general engagement in the north.

119

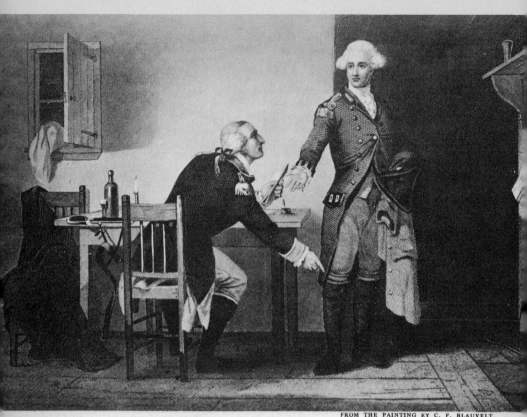

FROM THE PAINTING BY C. F. BLAUVELT.

ARNOLD'S TREASON

With the British holding New York, American control of the upper Hudson was essential. That control was West Point and the command of it was given Benedict Arnold. He was a brilliant officer and on his record should have held a position second only to that of Washington. But Congress had both harried him and promoted over him men of less ability. Stung to the quick, Arnold persuaded the young British officer Major André to carry plans of the defenses at West Point to Clinton, the British commander in New York.

LAST MOMENTS OF MAJOR ANDRÉ

André was captured near Sleepy Hollow, and the papers found in his boot. Hearing of his capture, Arnold escaped from West Point and later fought for the British. André was hung as a spy, an act which the British claimed was murder, saying he should have been treated as a prisoner of war. Had Arnold resigned from the army his worth undoubtedly would have been recognized, and that in his own lifetime. Tradition says that, years later, as he was dying in London he called for his faded American uniform saying, "May God forgive me for ever putting on any other."

CLARK AT KASKASKIA

George Rogers Clark is responsible for the winning of the northwest. "The Hannibal of the Missouri" is the historic name which he acquired by his conquest of what was then known as the Northwest Territory. With but two hundred men he took Kaskaskia and Vincennes in Illinois but was forced out of the latter place. The little army then marched back to Vincennes, sometimes wading through icy water that was neck deep. Clark's one chance was to take the fort before reënforcements would come to it in the spring. On February 24, 1779, the garrison was surprised. Clark's campaign pushed the British back to Detroit and made the western country safe for the rest of the war.

122

CAPTURING THE "SERAPIS"

John Paul Jones, commanding the *Bon Homme Richard*, closed with the British ship *Serapis* on September 23, 1779, and when asked if he was about to surrender called back, "I have not yet begun to fight." The deck of the *Serapis* was cleared of defenders and she was captured. Jones established the tradition of heroism in the American navy. Next to Jones's exploits, the most important naval battles of the Revolution were fought by the privateers. They did British shipping much damage.

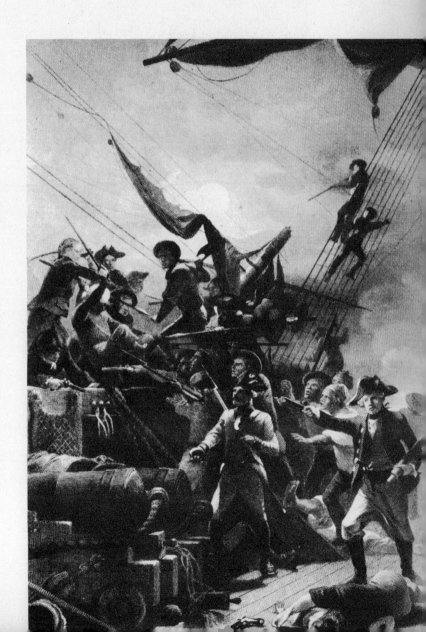

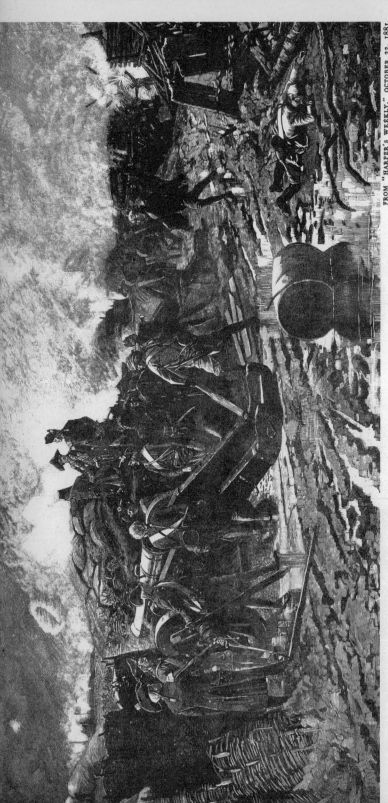

WASHINGTON IN THE TRENCHES AT YORKTOWN

FROM "HARPER'S WEEKLY," OCTOBER 22, 1881.

The British moved the war to the south in 1778 hoping to conquer the less solidly anti-Tory colonies and sweep north. This plan was ultimately unsuccessful. Wearied by long marches which won him small victories but no territory, Cornwallis at last retreated to Yorktown, Virginia. Now came to pass the opportunity so long awaited, to make use of the French fleet. De Grasse was prevailed on to cut off the possibility of either reënforcements or a retreat by water, French and American troops were hurried down from the north, and the "mouse trap" sprung.

SURRENDER AT YORKTOWN

Cornwallis was outnumbered two to one. About half of Washington's troops were French regulars. The end was inevitable. It came on October 17, 1781. When it was time to deliver up his sword on the 19th, Cornwallis pleaded illness and it was handed over by General O'Hara to General Lincoln who immediately handed it back to O'Hara. Everyone realized the war was over.

The peace treaty of 1783 recognized the independence of the United States with a boundary line, roughly stated, as the Mississippi, the middles of lakes Superior, Huron, Erie, and Ontario, the St. Lawrence, and then, with the exception of the northern part of Maine, the forty-fifth parallel to the coast. Spain held Florida.

WASHINGTON AS COMMANDER

Time and historical research have only verified the popular American belief that the war was won by George Washington. With an inferior force given to deserting him each year as winter came on, with jealousy and conspiracy often within his own staff, and with a Congress continually insolvent and hence unable to give him adequate support in men and supplies, he held steadfast before the finest troops in the British army for more than six years. It was a man, no sentimental story-book hero who did this. Around his genius as a commander (great, but not as great as some would have it), his fairness, his ability to inspire confidence, and above all his rare charm, the Revolutionary War was accomplished.

COURTESY OF THE MUSEUM OF FINE ARTS, BOSTON. FROM THE PAINTING BY JOHN SINGLETON COPLEY.

JOHN HANCOCK

John Hancock played a leading part in Massachusetts before, during, and after the Revolution. He was rich and possessed of a high social position. Therefore when he championed the cause of the radicals, his words carried more weight than did the opinions of less eminent men. He was for revolt from the beginning, played a large part in winning the reluctant ones over to the Declaration of Independence, and later became the first governor of his state. Although his purse stood to profit by independence, commercial motives alone did not dictate his fight for liberty.

SAMUEL ADAMS

Samuel Adams was the organizer, the firebrand, and the drill master of the Revolution. At the age of 21, on receiving his master's degree from Harvard, he sounded the keynote of the Revolution, and that was 36 years before the Declaration of Independence. He was among the first to propose independence, he continually opposed compromise with England, and he directed the Boston Tea Party. He was a supreme politician and a master of impassioned appeal. He and Hancock were warned of the intent of the British to arrest them at Lexington and escaped before the battle took place there. He based his faith on the common man and never faltered in that faith.

COURTESY OF THE MUSEUM OF FINE ARTS, BOSTON.   FROM THE PAINTING BY JOHN SINGLETON COPLEY.

PATRICK HENRY SPEAKING TO THE VIRGINIA ASSEMBLY

Patrick Henry, orator and statesman, was the idol of the common people of Virginia. Not quite as radical as the New Englanders, Adams and Hancock, he was yet one of the outstanding political figures of his day. As early as 1765 Patrick Henry stirred the House of Burgesses in aristocratic Virginia with his defense of the rights of British subjects and his defiant opposition to the Stamp Act. He ended his burst of oratory with the now famous words, "If that be treason, make the most of it." Standing in the doorway listening with rapt attention was a 22-year-old Virginian, Thomas Jefferson, who then and there was fired with the justness of the American cause and eleven years later wrote the Declaration of Independence. Patrick Henry has been aptly described by Claude G. Bowers as "the prophet, the phrase-maker, the orator, the trumpeter of revolt."

THOMAS PAINE: Pamphleteer

The idea of independence was at first foreign to the minds of the mass of American colonists. They struggled during the early years of the Revolution only for what they conceived to be their inalienable rights as English subjects. The popular movement for independence, the movement which converted the people generally to this radical step can, however, be dated from the publication of the little pamphlet *Common Sense* in 1776, written by Thomas Paine. Thousands read its simple, easy-to-understand words, and Washington himself paid tribute to its widespread effect. Paine's earlier and also tremendously successful pamphlet, *The Crisis*, had begun with the famous words, "These are the times that try men's souls."

THE ADOPTION OF THE DECLARATION

On June 7, 1776, Richard Henry Lee on behalf of Virginia offered the resolution "that these United Colonies are, and of right ought to be, free and independent states." John Adams seconded on behalf of Massachusetts. On June 11th Benjamin Franklin, John Adams, Roger Sherman, Robert R. Livingston, and Thomas Jefferson were chosen as a committee to prepare a Declaration. Though he was only 33 years of age and the youngest member of the committee, Jefferson received the most votes and therefore became the chairman. The committee left the task entirely to him and he wrote it at a single sitting without reference to any book or memoranda. Franklin and Adams then made a few slight alterations and then the committee presented it to Congress on June 28. The debate continued throughout the 2nd, 3rd, and 4th of July, when it was finally adopted and as Jefferson wrote in his memoirs, "signed by every member present except Mr. Dickinson." However, the only signed Declaration known to us was engrossed later and signed on August 2, 1776. This document bears the signatures of some who became members of the Congress after July 4th and it lacks the signatures of a few of those who voted for adoption.

READING THE DECLARATION OUTSIDE THE STATE HOUSE

"All men are created equal," "Life, Liberty and the pursuit of Happiness," "free and independent," "pledge . . . our Lives, our Fortunes, and our sacred Honour." Such were the words below which John Hancock was the first to place his name. As news of the Declaration spread throughout the colonies, many marked the event with public celebration, but others were left sobered and thoughtful by the solemnity of the words they read and the finality of the step that had at last been taken. There could be no turning back now.

131

Entered according to Act of Congress in the year 1874, by Davis Garber, in the office of the Librarian of Congress at Washington, D. C.

Independence Hall, Philadelphia, on the Eve of July 4th, 1776.

Explanation.—It is sunset on the 4th of July, 1776. The members of the Old Continental Congress, having signed the Declaration, are seen in the act of leaving the Hall of Independence. Hancock, distinguished by his dark dress, stands on the steps in front of the hall-door, announcing to a friend that the Declaration has just been signed. Franklin is seen at his right, Jefferson leans against the right pillar of the door. Adams is conversing with Jefferson—between their heads is seen the face of Livingston—and against the left pillar stands Roger Sherman. These form the group on the steps. We then commence on the left of the picture, and counting every figure, discover the following persons : 1, a citizen ; 2, Wilson, a signer ; 3, a citizen ; 4, a tory ; 5, a signer ; 6, a lady ; 7, her father ; 8, the Indian who bore the Declaration to the camp of Washington ; 9, Thomas Paine, talking with No. 10, Benjamin Rush, and 11, Robert Morris, both signers. Behind them the heads of citizens are and to the right, a crowd of patriots, Quakers, tories, &c., eagerly disputing the na and merits of the Declaration

BETSY ROSS AND THE FLAG

The popularly believed story of the origin of the first flag is open to very serious doubts. Betsy Ross was an upholsterer in Philadelphia. The story is that Washington and George Ross came to her asking if she would make a flag. They showed her a design, decided on five-pointed instead of six-pointed stars, and later sent her a colored design, following which she sewed together the flag. Certain it is that it was not until June 14, 1777, that Congress declared the flag should have thirteen stripes, alternate red and white, and thirteen white stars on a blue field.

FRANKLIN AT THE FRENCH COURT

Franklin, during the war, was sent by Congress to secure aid from France. The task was far from easy. He, a Protestant, at a Catholic court, was appealing to a sovereign to help a group of rebels overturn their own legitimate sovereign. In addition, the colonies had been the enemies of France for a century and a half, but the desire to check the increasing power of Britain prevailed and Franklin completed his mission, securing men, money, and ships. He became extremely popular in Paris (shopkeepers ran out to see him as he passed down the street), he went to Versailles frequently, and was received by Louis XVI and Marie Antoinette. When he died in Philadelphia in 1790, the French assembly went into mourning for three days.

THE FOUNDATION OF AMERICAN GOVERNMENT

SIGNING THE CONSTITUTION

When the war ended, far-sighted men soon began to realize that there was need for a stronger tie between the states. After four years of increasing financial embarrassment, difficulties as to commerce, and the appearance of unrest in some of the states, a group of conservative leaders arranged for the calling of a Constitutional Convention in Philadelphia in 1787. To it were sent, fortunately, the most able statesmen and leaders of the day. Washington presided, the venerable Franklin was present, and both exercised great influence. The opposition was fearful for the rights of the states. After violent controversy and many compromises the present Constitution was the result. The success and final accord "is one of the miracles of history. It was due to the genius and patriotism of a few men, and among these the foremost was James Madison." His own contemporaries gratefully named him "Father of the Constitution." On September 17, 1787, thirty-nine of the fifty-five delegates signed. But their action was taken in the name of the states present, i. e., represented.

CELEBRATING THE CONSTITUTION IN NEW YORK

Having won equal representation in the Senate, most of the small states hurried to adopt the Constitution. Two of the largest, New York and Virginia, lagged. Without them the union would indeed have been weak. Madison led the fight for adoption in Virginia and Hamilton in New York. In New York *The Federalist* papers, a series of essays explaining the Constitution, did much to win the popular vote, and finally she ratified in July, 1788. In the city there was a huge celebration parade in which moved the ship *Hamilton*, named for the chief author of *The Federalist*. When Rhode Island ratified in 1790, a stable form of government had at last been set up in America.

WASHINGTON INAUGURATED

It was the unanimous opinion of the country that Washington should be the first president. Only with reluctance did he accept the honor. His journey from Virginia to New York for the inauguration was a triumphal procession. He was sworn in on April 30, 1789, on the balcony of Federal Hall. Although perhaps not a great statesman he commanded, however, universal respect and was able to prevent the country from splitting into violent factions in the first critical years of its existence.

136

HUNTERS AND TRAPPERS

The hunter and the trapper have become symbols in our history. These people, in the vanguard of civilization, pushed the frontier across the Alleghenies, then to the Mississippi, to the Missouri, to the Rockies, to the great northwest, and to the Pacific. Carrying what little they owned in the world on their backs, they departed from their homes, leaving their more settled countrymen to struggle with the problem of turning thirteen loosely bound colonies into a united nation.

THE PIONEER WEST

The pioneers, who followed in the footsteps of the early hunters, brought their families with them. Their wives, after braving the hardships of the outward journey, settled down to make homes in the rude cabins their husbands built. They ate of the scanty food, did the cooking, made the family clothes, helped to fight off the Indians, thought little of raising families of ten children, and all this in continual poverty. Such was the caliber of the American pioneer stock. Who can say that they were not happy?

138

DANIEL BOONE: LEADING A PARTY THROUGH THE CUMBERLAND GAP

Daniel Boone has become the exemplar of the hunter-pioneer type—brave, resourceful, kindly, and always restless in the settlements. His life illustrates the era of westward expansion before and after the Revolution. In the spring of 1769 he stood gazing down on "his" Kentucky. Under the direction of Richard Henderson and Co., he helped to defend and establish the settle-ment of Kentucky. But the lands he chose for himself among his neighbors were, in the end, taken away from him because of a technical flaw in the legal title. Hence in 1799, when he was sixty-five, he left Kentucky again for the west. Far away on the Missouri River and alone once more he made his last home.

FROM A PAINTING BY CHARLES M. RUSSELL. COURTESY MONTANA HISTORICAL SOCIETY.

LEWIS AND CLARK: MEETING WITH THE SHOSHONES

Captain Meriweather Lewis and Lieutenant William Clark were the first to reach the Pacific by crossing the continent north of Mexico. One was the brother of George Rogers Clark, "The Hannibal of the Missouri," and the other was secretary to Thomas Jefferson, who inspired, counseled, and partially financed the expedition so that the recently acquired Louisiana Territory might be extended to the far northwest; assuring the American people a vast empire stretching from the Atlantic to the Pacific; wiping out the danger of conflicting bordering nations like those that have caused constant wars in Europe. They started from St. Louis in 1804 with the definite task of getting accurate information about the land and the Indians to the west. They made the difficult ascent of the Missouri River, crossed the Rockies, and then descended the Columbia River system to the ocean. Their discoveries constituted our most important claim to the Oregon territory.

140

ESTABLISHING TERRITORIAL GOVERNMENT AT MARIETTA

In 1787 Congress provided for a territorial government northeast of the Ohio River. Among other things this Ordinance, drawn by Thomas Jefferson, declared that slavery would not be tolerated therein. The Ordinance became the model for the other territories and states which were to come into being in the west. Immigrants at first came slowly into Ohio, but when the government opened new land offices in 1800 and allowed settlers to buy on credit at $2 per acre as little as 320 acres, the flood began.

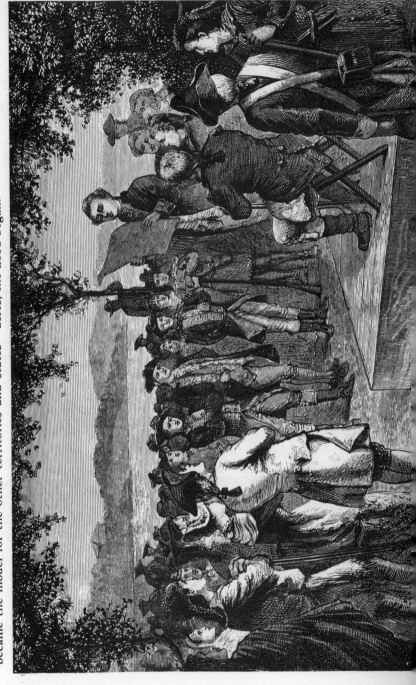

THE FUR TRADE: SURRENDER OF ASTORIA

The fur trade was a potent factor in opening up the Far West, just as it had been in the East. John Jacob Astor, a New York capitalist, attempted to organize this trade. He planned to have his American Fur Company dominate the Great Lakes, the Western plains, and the northwest. His settlement at Astoria on the Columbia River failed. When the War of 1812 approached he sold out his property rights to the Northwest Company of Canada, and a little later a British squadron captured the settlement, but it was restored to the United States after the war. The other two ventures added to Astor's already large fortune.

SANTA FÉ TRADE

The route from St. Louis to Independence, and thence across Kansas to Santa Fé (the Santa Fé Trail), sprang into life after Mexico revolted from Spain. Cotton cloth and other manufactured articles were carried out to the Indians. Furs came back. The trade lasted up to the war with Mexico. Although there was ruthless competition between the traders, they banded together in caravans while crossing the Indian-infested country of Kansas.

FROM A PAINTING BY ALLEN TRUE IN THE PUBLIC LIBRARY, DENVER.

FROM "HARPER'S WEEKLY," FOR SEPTEMBER 4, 1858.

THE MORMONS AT SALT LAKE: THE DESERET STORE

In 1847 the Mormons (Latter-Day Saints) arrived on the shores of Salt Lake, Utah. There Brigham Young, his authority absolute, sought to set up his empire. More than 15,000 came to his tiny city. While the element of polygamy has received popular attention it must be remembered that Young was one of the great colonizers of history because by irrigation he made the desert produce. Furthermore, the stores which the Mormons set up, such as this one at Salt Lake City, did a thriving business with the weary California-seekers. In the latter part of the 19th century the Mormons made permanent peace with the United States and abandoned the practise of polygamy.

SETTLEMENT OF CALIFORNIA

As late as 1750 there was little knowledge of California. Spain had long occupied Lower California but it was 1769 before a real attempt was made at colonization to the north, and then mostly through the missions which grew to dominate both the Indians and the economic life of the country. After California broke with Spain in 1822 the missions were secularized. In the years before the Mexican War, Americans began moving in in large numbers, to trade and to find homes.

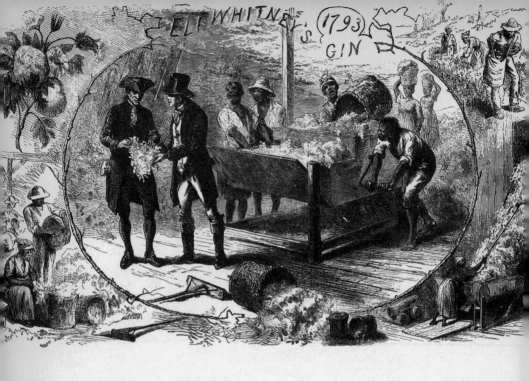

THE COTTON GIN

In 1793 Eli Whitney invented the cotton gin, a hand-operated contrivance for separating short staple cotton from its seeds. This machine transformed a part of our economic life. It made it possible for cotton-growing to flourish in the South, gave life to a social system centering around great estates, added another export crop to Southern agriculture, and made slavery a permanent institution. Slavery and cotton were the answers to the problem of developing the post-Revolution South.

146

THE ERIE CANAL

The nation and its goods moved along roads in the years immediately after the Revolution. In the 1820's and 1830's, however, water transportation was on the increase. It was the success of the Erie Canal from Buffalo to New York which after 1825 gave the "Canal Era" its impetus and lifted New York to economic leadership. Many cities sought to benefit themselves by building canals. The railroad put an end to the great era of canal construction.

FULTON'S "CLERMONT"

Our natural waterways began to play their great part in American history
with the coming of the steamboat. Robert Fulton's *Clermont* chugged out
into the Hudson River in 1807 amid the cheers of a crowd that had come to
jeer at the inventor and his "folly." Fulton put nothing new into the steamboat. His great achievement was to assemble for successful commercial
use parts which others had developed. In providing cheap transportation
his invention had enormous economic implications.

COMING OF THE RAILROADS: THE FIRST TRAIN IN PENNSYLVANIA

The railroad was destined to have the greatest effect of all on our economic life. The locomotive, an English invention, began to supplant horses on American railroads in the early 1830's. First the Baltimore & Ohio experimented, then the Charleston & Hamburg, and then the Mohawk & Hudson. As the success of this new means of transportation became apparent many small roads sprang up all over the country. After the Civil War began the era of consolidation.

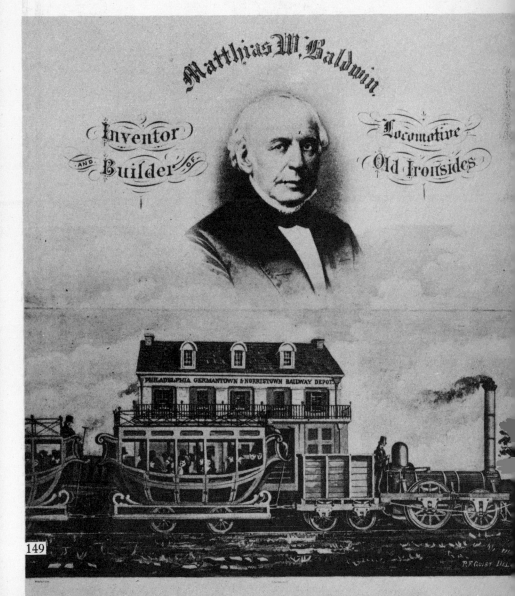

149

FIRST RAILWAY TRAIN IN PENNSYLVANIA,

Drawn by "Old Ironsides" on the Phila., Germ. & Norr. R. R.

AGE OF THE CLIPPERS:

THE "FLYING CLOUD"

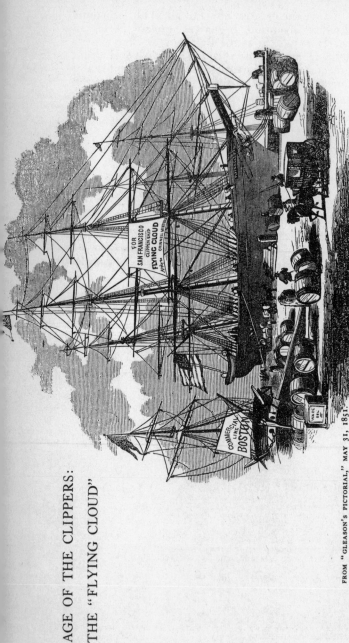

FROM "GLEASON'S PICTORIAL," MAY 31, 1851.

Americans had always known how to build good boats and sail them, but after the War of 1812 American ships began to be a force in world trade. The financial success of the lines operating packets, ships that sailed on a regular schedule, worked this change. They captured the cream of the Atlantic trade. But competition was stiff and the cry was for more speed and yet more speed. In 1845 John Willis Griffiths gave his answer. He launched the first clipper, the *Rainbow*. On her initial voyage to China she not only paid for herself but re-turned her owners a profit equal to her cost. Griffiths became a hero. One of the greatest clippers ever built was John McKay's *Flying Cloud*. She reached San Francisco in eighty-nine days, a record never beaten by a sailing vessel. The record for a clipper's single day's run was and still is 436 miles, made by *Lightning*, a mark that rivals many modern steamers. The years of the clippers marked the zenith of our merchant marine. In their day the finest ships the world had ever seen flew the American flag.

150

GROWTH OF NEW YORK: BROADWAY AT ST. PAUL'S CHURCH, 1831

Our cities were the first to feel the effects of the changes wrought by the new inventions, the cheaper transportation, and the spread of our population. As one instance, the Erie Canal may be cited. Its opening in 1825 marked the beginning of modern New York as a financial and industrial center. Such things were an indication of the tremendously important fact that the country's economic prosperity was beginning to find a basis in pursuits other than those of agriculture.

GROWTH OF CHICAGO: THE FIRST SHIPMENT OF WHEAT

The decade of the 1830's witnessed Chicago's birth as a city. A tiny village in 1830, by 1840 she had seen her destiny clearly. From her harbor her first shipment of wheat, seventy-eight bushels, was sent in 1838. A rail-road connection with the East in 1852 gave her a firm grip on the already enormous lake trade and helped to establish her as the center of a fertile territory rich in natural resources.

THE AGRICULTURAL SOUTH

In the years before the Civil War the South developed its unique social system. The great slave-owning planters, who were but a fraction of the white population, dominated this system. Next was the great bulk of the white population, who owned their farms but few slaves.

The slave population grew from about 650,000 in 1790 to almost four million in 1860. By and large the South shared in the economic progress of the rest of the country.

GROWTH OF ORGANIZED RELIGION

The first years of the 19th century witnessed a revival of the religious spirit. The English church, loyal during the Revolution, was reorganized on an American basis. The Methodists spread rapidly through the work of the itinerant preachers. Puritanism was disintegrating by 1800 and from its ashes eventually rose the Unitarians and other sects that dissented from the old form. The period also witnessed the rise of the camp meeting, that unique American institution. It became a powerful influence in the religious life of the rural sections. The illustration shows the Old North Church in Boston, one of the most famous of the early New England places of worship.

154

GROWTH OF ORGANIZED EDUCATION

The much-prized system of public schools, so universal today did not come into existence at an early date. In Virginia a state-wide school system was proposed in 1779 by Thomas Jefferson in his "Bill for the General Diffusion of Knowledge," but it was not until 1825 that he succeeded with a part of the program with the opening of the University of Virginia. In Massachusetts it was not until the work of Horace Mann, during the 1840's, that education became universally available. The middle states between 1815 and 1860 gradually perfected school systems, but in the South good schools for everyone did not come until after the Civil War. However, there was wide public education almost from the first in the West. The period witnessed the rise of the Academy, the founding of many colleges and universities, and the beginning of the great state university system, first in the South, then in the Southwest and West.

THE FIRST TESTING OF THE McCORMICK REAPER

Cyrus McCormick perfected a reaper in 1834. After ventures first in New York and then in Ohio he began to realize that the tiny city of Chicago was the key to the vast grain fields of the prairies where the market existed for his invention. To that city he moved in 1847 and began selling his machine on the installment plan, an idea almost as revolutionary as the invention itself. The reaper gave the Mid-West farmer his place in the economic sun and his fields became the granary for both this country and a large part of Europe.

156

THE MORSE TELEGRAPH

Samuel F. B. Morse made the first telegraph instrument in 1836 but it was not until several years later that the doubting world gave him a chance to show what he had done. Meanwhile, he suffered poverty and rebuffs here and abroad. At last Congress passed an appropriation with which a telegraph line was built from Baltimore to Washington. On May 24, 1844, the famous message, "What hath God wrought," was tapped out and the instantaneous transfer of human thought became an accomplished fact.

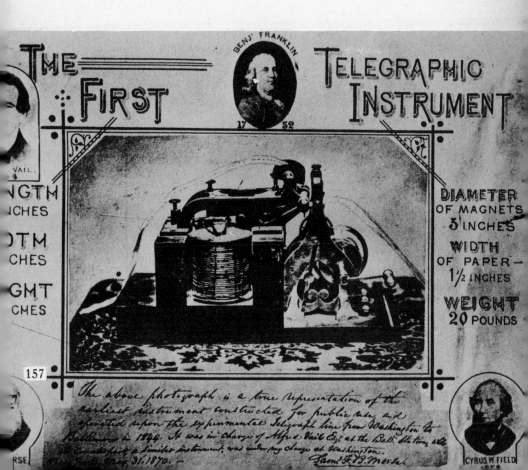

DIGGING GOLD IN CALIFORNIA

The story of the gold rush to California in 1849 and 1850 is the story of a country gone crazy. News of the first discovery turned San Francisco into a deserted city almost over night. Five hundred ships soon lay in the harbor without sailors, and newspapers suspended publication because there were no typesetters. More than twenty thousand persons set out overland from the east, suffering innumerable hardships and risking life itself in the search for easy riches. Thousands more arrived by water.

FROM "BALLOU'S PICTORIAL DRAWING-ROOM COMPANION" FOR MAY 3, 1856.

158

JENNY LIND SINGING IN CASTLE GARDEN

Jenny Lind was almost unknown here when P. T. Barnum, hearing of the furore she had created in London, decided to risk his fortune and bring the "Swedish Nightingale" to New York. Her first concert at Castle Garden, in September, 1850, was attended by a huge crowd. On learning that someone once paid $225 for a ticket she wrote home naïvely, "It is amazing what heaps of money they have here." Almost every appearance during her tour of our cities was in the nature of a civic event.

THE "AMERICA" READY FOR LAUNCHING

In 1851 the schooner *America* sailed for England to accept a challenge that had been sent to American sportsmen by the Royal Yacht Squadron. She had been built by a syndicate of New York yachtsmen. On August 22nd she beat seventeen of the fastest boats in England on the difficult course around the Isle of Wight, her nearest competitor being twenty-four minutes behind. The cup that the *America* won has been successfully defended for almost eighty-five years against all comers.

FROM "GLEASON'S PICTORIAL" FOR MAY 31, 1851.

PERRY OPENS JAPAN

In 1854 Japan, sleeping in self-imposed isolation since time immemorial, was opened to the world by Commodore Matthew C. Perry of the American navy. Perry, backed by six vessels and bearing a letter from President Fillmore, concluded with the *shogun* our first treaty with Japan. This provided, among other things, that our ships should be permitted to trade in two ports and that privileges allowed other countries must thereafter be accorded to us. The photograph, taken at Washington in 1860, shows the first Japanese embassy to the United States.

161

FROM "HARPER'S WEEKLY" FOR SEPTEMBER 11, 1858.

THE ATLANTIC CABLE

Cyrus W. Field's attempt to lay an Atlantic cable in 1857 failed. In 1858, after another failure, his two ships met in midocean and, splicing a new cable, one sailed for Europe and one for America. Tremendous celebrations followed when the vessels reached shore. This contemporary drawing shows a miniature *Niagara*, one of the cable ships, being paraded in triumph on Broadway in New York. Field's joy was short-lived, for a month later the wire ceased to carry messages. Success, however, was ultimately attained in 1866.

THE PONY EXPRESS

The short-lived Pony Express is one of the most picturesque episodes in our history. It started April 3, 1860, between St. Joseph, Missouri, and Sacramento, California, a journey which it made in eleven days. Men changed horses every twenty-five miles and each man made three stages, except when Indians or bad weather forced a different schedule. As the telegraph lines advanced, the Pony Express cut down its run, and when the wires were joined in 1862 it became a memory.

THE FIRST BANK OF THE UNITED STATES

The first Bank of the United States, begun by Hamilton in Washington's first administration, occupied this building after 1796. The bank's charter had been the foundation for the famous controversy between Jefferson and Hamilton over the construction of the powers of Congress under the Constitution. The bank continued until 1811. Its charter expired in that year. The attempts to renew the charter brought about some of the political battles of President Jackson's administration.

164

THE FEDERALISTS AND THE REPUBLICANS

The campaign of 1796 was the first in which there had been a contest for the Presidency. It was marked by bitter party strife between Washington's Federalist Party and the Republican opposition. John Adams, a Federalist and a keen student of government but a poor politician, was elected. Thomas Jefferson, receiving the second largest number of votes, became Vice-President. He was the leader of the Republicans. The difficulties of domestic politics were aggravated by the fact that England and France were at war and that the government of the United States was thought by the French government to be bound to it by the treaty of 1778. James Monroe, appointed by Washington as minister to France, nevertheless sympathized with the views of Jefferson and his party and was, therefore, greatly embarrassed by the negotiation by Mr. Jay of the treaty of 1794 with Great Britain, which was, of course, most unpopular in Paris. Towards the end of Washington's administration Monroe was recalled and Charles Cotesworth Pinckney was sent over. But he was refused permission to reside in France. In the administration of John Adams the Federalists heard of this rebuff and became loud in their cry for war. Finally, after Pinckney had been succeeded by a commission and that commission had met in France offers of bribery, even some Republicans joined the Federalists in the popular slogan of the day, "Millions for defense, but not one cent for tribute." (The above illustration, which is contemporary, pictures the Federalist point of view in the controversy.) But Adams was able to restrain the hot-headed ones in both parties, partly due to the fact that France herself did not desire war. The differences were finally patched up in 1800, but party conflict had been intensified by the affair and in 1801 Jefferson, the first of the Virginia Dynasty, a believer in the common people and a clever politician, became President. The Federalist Party now entered upon its progressive decline.

THE WHISKY REBELLION

The Whisky Rebellion is significant because it came as a result of the first attempt to enforce federal laws in the states. In 1791 Congress had placed an excise tax on spirits, which the local whisky distillers in Pennsylvania resented. Violence began in 1794, and some federal officers who attempted to collect the tax were tarred and feathered. The 15,000 troops that Washington requested were more than enough to suppress the revolt, and this unneeded demonstration of power caused wide resentment against the Federalist party. Some said that Alexander Hamilton deliberately forced the tax as a test of federal strength.

JAY'S TREATY OF 1795

John Jay was sent by Washington to London to endeavor to settle the problems which had developed in our relations with Great Britain as a result of the outbreak of the great European war that followed the French Revolution. These problems included the searching of American ships on the seas, and the abandonment of the English outposts in the west, held by the British in violation of the treaty of 1783. The treaty he brought back, although it averted war and settled the question of the western posts, failed to reach a desirable settlement of the West India trade problem. It caused resentment against the Federalists. Jay was burned in effigy in many cities. The election of 1796 was, accordingly, a close one. Washington retired from office with his famous plea for freedom from European entanglement. John Adams became President.

THOMAS JEFFERSON AND THE REPUBLICANS

In 1801 the long reign of the Federalists came to an end with the election of Thomas Jefferson. Although a Virginia aristocrat, he however knew the reactions of the mass as Washington, Hamilton, and Adams had not. His principles of human rights, equality, economy, and states rights have become so fundamental in American politics that no wise candidate since his time has dared ignore them in word, however much they may have been able to avoid them in deed or by subterfuge.

CELEBRATING THE PURCHASE OF LOUISIANA

The greatest achievement of Jefferson's administration was the purchase from Napoleon of the Louisiana territory in 1803. By it our domain was increased by 140%. The acquisition made the entire Mississippi Valley completely ours and included most or all of thirteen future states. All possibility of war on our western border was abolished and the nation at last became free to exploit the vast territories and immense wealth of the country dominated by the mighty Mississippi.

169

THE BURR–HAMILTON DUEL

Aaron Burr, originally a Republican, joined the extreme Federalist party in New York in the campaign of 1804 and so became party to an ill-starred plan to split off the northern colonies from the union. Alexander Hamilton, a Federalist himself, but loyal, bestirred himself to defeat his traditional opponent. Burr, after the election, demanded satisfaction for some of the charges made against him in the campaign, and the famous duel was the result. Hamilton was killed and Burr fled for his life.

BURR ADDRESSING HIS ARMY

In 1805 Burr made his first journey to the west. Later, on the Ohio River, he began to hatch a scheme which was aimed either to establish a state of his own in Louisiana or to make an attack on Mexico. Just what he had in mind we may never know. In November, 1806, Jefferson ordered his arrest on the charge of treason, and his trial was the most sensational the country has ever witnessed. It was really a contest between Chief Justice John Marshall who presided, and who wished to establish the power of the federal courts at the expense of the executive, and Jefferson. Jefferson won, despite the fact that Burr was acquitted.

INFLUENCE OF JOHN MARSHALL

John Marshall dominated the Supreme Court from 1801 to 1835. In a series
of famous cases he moulded the Constitution in its most plastic days along
conservative lines. He gave to the federal government much-needed
strength, and weakened the doctrine of states rights. Time and again the
people showed at the polls that their views were not those of the Chief
Justice, but he ignored them and by so doing strengthened the Constitution
as the basis of our national life.

172

MISSOURI COMPROMISE: RUFUS KING

Everything seemed peaceful in the Republican administration of Monroe (the fifth held by the "Virginia Dynasty" of Jefferson, Madison, and Monroe), until the suggestion was made that slavery be barred from the proposed state of Missouri. Instantly pandemonium broke loose. Finally, a compromise which it was hoped would settle the slavery question for all time, was agreed on in 1820. Missouri should come in without restriction, but henceforth slavery should be prohibited north of Missouri's southern boundary in the rest of the Louisiana Purchase. At the same time Maine was admitted, which helped satisfy the North. Rufus King, one of the recognized leaders of the Federalist Party, was an outstanding figure in the senate debates on the Compromise, supporting the anti-slavery side of the argument.

173

JAMES MONROE: THE MONROE DOCTRINE

The Monroe Doctrine came partly as result of the vaguely formed desire in Europe to regain for Spain her South American colonies. This did not suit England's ambitions and she suggested that we join in preventing it. Monroe had the sound advice of Thomas Jefferson and of John Quincy Adams, Monroe's Secretary of State; they had far too much sense to fall for any such scheme. Monroe announced in 1823 the so-called Monroe Doctrine. It embodied three ideas. First, we intend taking no part in European domestic troubles; second, Europe's political system, being different from ours, we would view as an unfriendly act any attempt to extend that system to American states which have established their independence; third, the American continents are not "subjects for future colonization by any European powers." This third principle was evoked by the threat of Russian expansion on the coast.

174

THE RISE OF THE TARIFF

With the act passed in 1816, the tariff became one of the battlegrounds of American politics. In 1824 a relatively moderate measure was passed due to the fact that some New England states were still anti-tariff. But in 1828 this division between the northern states had largely disappeared and with this unanimity a higher tariff wall was raised. The subject was soon a national issue, with the South in revolt. Calhoun became its spokesman in a movement which had important implications. The picture shows the Coffee-House Slip at the foot of Wall Street, New York, into whose harbor was already beginning to move the commerce of the world.

175

FROM THE PAINTING BY G. A. HEALY IN FANEUIL HALL, BOSTON.

WEBSTER'S REPLY TO HAYNE

Calhoun became the chief sponsor of the doctrine of nullification, that is, that a state has the right to ignore the acts of Congress when that state deems them passed outside the powers granted by the Constitution or passed to affect but one section of the country. In 1830, as a result of a proposed limitation on the sale of public lands, Robert Y. Hayne, of Calhoun's own state of South Carolina, rose to defend the doctrine of nullifica-tion and states rights. He represented the flower of Southern oratory. A few days later, Daniel Webster of Massachusetts rose in reply. The gallery was crowded as he delivered one of the most masterly defenses of the Constitution ever conceived. After that, the debate subsided. Not even the most far-sighted men of the day saw that the issue was not settled.

176

ANDREW JACKSON'S "EXPERIMENT"

With the advent of Andrew Jackson in 1829 came "Jacksonian Democracy." He believed that the government had been run by the few for their own profit and set about to right the matter. The mass of the people was to be relied on. As a result of championing their cause, the people in their turn became suddenly willing to turn over to him immense powers of government. President Jackson's opponents called him "King Andrew," and claimed that the people were really robbing themselves. The cartoon, expressing the opposition to Jackson, shows the President as complete master of his ship. One of the sailors is saying, of the ship in the background, "There is the old *Constitution* burning up —Her owners having no further occasion for her and can't afford to keep her in repair."

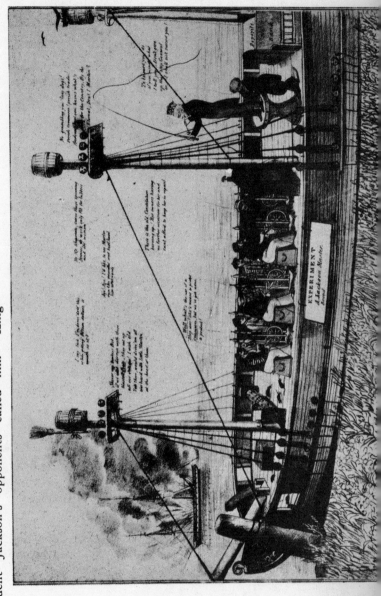

THE SECOND BANK OF THE UNITED STATES

The charter of the first Bank of the United States, which had rendered yeoman service in straightening out our tangled financial affairs after the period of the Confederation, expired in 1811 and was refused renewal. In 1815 Madison, a Republican, asked for its re-establishment. It was said that he was out-Federalizing Federalism, for Jefferson had been most forceful, to Washington, in his opposition to the first charter. Monroe, the last of the Virginia Dynasty, followed Madison and under him the Bank prospered. However, in the first administration of Jackson, the Bank became the center of one of the severest political controversies in our history. Jackson, "the People's Champion," viewed the Bank as one manifestation of the power of the few over the many and he set out to destroy it. He accomplished this first, by vetoing a bill for the rechartering of the Bank and, secondly, by the simple method of not depositing any more funds in the Bank and by gradually withdrawing present governmental funds to state banks. (See the illustration, a contemporary cartoon.) In the controversy, Jackson was pitted against Nicholas Biddle, of Philadelphia, President of the Bank. Jackson was completely triumphant, and when the Bank's charter expired in 1836 it was forced to become a state bank. A chain of events following the end of the Bank and the distribution of the Treasury surplus, including the inflation of state bank notes, speculation especially in government lands, and finally the Specie Circular which required that all payments to the government be made in national currency, marked the prelude to the severe panic of 1837.

Draw'd off from Natur by Zek Downing, Neffu to Major Jack Downing.

THE DOWNFALL OF MOTHER BANK.

HENRY CLAY: THE "FORCE BILL"

In pursuance of the doctrine of nullification South Carolina by ordinance of her convention in 1832 declared the federal tariff acts not binding on her. The situation became threatening when Jackson sent to Congress a bill empowering the President to enforce federal laws with the army and the navy. Henry Clay now removed South Carolina's objection by securing the adoption of a bill to reduce gradually the tariff. Having won her point, that state agreed to repeal her ordinance. Nullification was at an end. The country breathed easily again.

THE PANIC OF 1837

The panic of 1837 was one of those recurrent crises, the causes of which are still disputed. As is always the case, partisan efforts sought to blame the hard times on the party in power. In 1837, especially, the international aspects and influences were largely overlooked. One of Jackson's policies which later became an object of attack was specie payment. When it became obvious that paper issued by the state banks, which the government had received in payment for lands in the West, would not be redeemed in specie, Jackson ordered the government's land banks to receive no more of it. The collapse of the speculation in Western lands was one of the manifestations of the panic. The illustration is from one of the specie cartoons of the period immediately after 1837.

180

"TIPPECANOE AND TYLER TOO"

Jackson forced Van Buren on his party in 1836. No sooner had the latter become President than the panic of 1837 engulfed him. Failure of Van Buren really to cope with it accomplished his defeat in 1840. The Whig candidate, Harrison, the hero of Tippecanoe, won easily with Tyler as running mate, on the famous slogan, "Tippecanoe and Tyler Too." But in little more than a month after he took office he died, and Tyler, a Jeffersonian Republican, became President. The cartoon illustrates the popular conception of the result on election day.

THE ANNEXATION OF TEXAS

The election of 1844 turned largely on the question of the annexation of Texas. The Democrats, with Polk as a candidate, favored it. The Whigs opposed it, with Clay as their leader. Northern dislike of the spread of slavery in so great a territory figured largely. Polk's election decided the issue, and Tyler hurried to secure the new state, which accepted the terms offered in the last days of 1845. Mexico meantime declared that the admission of Texas would be equivalent to a declaration of war. The cartoon shows Polk welcoming Texas, with Clay protesting.

THE TARIFF AND THE ELECTION OF 1844

The tariff was another of the battlegrounds of the bitter and exciting campaign of 1844. In Pennsylvania, Polk was openly accused of being a free trader. He cleverly answered this charge by saying he favored a tariff that would yield enough revenue for government expenses, if economically managed. This pleased the South and held protectionist Pennsylvania to her traditional political faith, for the tariff of 1842 had been passed to help defray government expenses. Pennsylvania Democrats campaigned for Polk on the slogan pictured in the cartoon.

183

THE OREGON QUESTION: A CARTOON

The westward spread of the population made the question of our right to Oregon an issue in the early 1840's. In pursuance of an agreement made in 1818 the territory had been occupied jointly by England and the United States, but in 1844 the West adopted the slogan, "Fifty-four forty or fight." It referred to the parallel up to which the extremists felt we had claim. England now compromised on a boundary along the forty-ninth parallel, the present line, and a settlement was made on this basis in 1846. Vancouver Island, in its entirety, went to Great Britain.

184

CALIFORNIA AND CLAY'S COMPROMISE

The rapid development of California and the rise there of a demand for statehood found Congress unable to pass necessary legislation by reason of unwillingness of Southerners to accept the Wilmot Proviso, which would exclude slavery. There arose danger of a secession movement, to avoid which Clay, whose powers for com- promise had previously been manifested, brought forth conciliatory proposals in his Omnibus Bill of 1850. This was unsuccessful, but the same principles were enacted in separate laws. The tendency to disunion was postponed.

185

THE STRUGGLE FOR CANADA: CAPTURE OF FORT GEORGE

England had been high-handed in searching American vessels seeking to
trade with the French, but this could have been settled amicably had not
the West cast loving eyes on Canada and the fur trade. Madison yielded.
We were forced to surrender Detroit in 1812 and then in early 1813, pur-
suing the campaign with more vigor, captured Fort George on Lake Ontario.
Our opening move in the War of 1812 was against Canada.

BATTLE OF CHIPPEWA

The balance of the year 1813, although it brought victory at the battle of the Thames under Harrison of Tippecanoe fame, and the recapture of Detroit, did not lead to general victory. In July, 1814, two victories, one at Chippewa and the other at Lundy's Lane, were won but the campaign against Canada was abandoned. The treasury was now bankrupt and there was little public enthusiasm for Madison's war.

PERRY AT THE BATTLE OF LAKE ERIE

Naval victory on Lake Erie played no small part in the Canadian campaign. No progress could be made on land until the control of the water was established. On September 10, 1813, Captain Oliver H. Perry defeated an inferior British fleet, despite the fact that he lost his flagship the *Lawrence* and was only able to renew the fight after being rowed across to the *Niagara*. His brief message to Harrison, "We have met the enemy and they are ours," has become a classic in American naval history.

BATTLE OF PLATTSBURG

In 1814 the British began the invasion of the Lake Champlain country. On September 11th the two fleets met, while the land forces awaited the outcome. The American commander Thomas MacDonough now won the most daring naval victory of the war. By it he made safe an entire section of the frontier from invasion and quite counterbalanced British successes around the Niagara and the coast of Maine.

THE "CONSTITUTION" AND THE "GUERRIÈRE"

The history of the War of 1812 should have taught us for all time the futility of a tiny navy, however efficient, in protecting a great coast line. The series of thrilling naval duels between the frigates in which we carried off the honors, including the victory of the mighty *Constitution* over the *Guerrière* on August 19, 1812, and the defeat of Lawrence in the *Chesapeake* ("Don't give up the ship"), had little effect on the outcome of the war. The weight of the British navy accomplished the blockade in 1813 and from that time on our navy was ineffectual.

AMERICAN PRIVATEERS: THE "CHASSEUR" AND THE "ST. LAWRENCE"

War was no sooner declared than American privateers were in action. These rough-and-ready individualists effectively harassed British shipping, seizing prizes to a value of almost $40,000,000. One of their most dramatic duels was that between the *Chasseur* and the British warship *St. Lawrence*, near Havana, in which the latter was taken in fifteen minutes. They rendered great service but they drew many fine seamen from the navy and never coöperated for any general purpose such as the lifting of the blockade. This war was the last in which we resorted to their use.

THE BURNING OF WASHINGTON

The British in 1814 sent an expedition against Washington and Baltimore. They met but a few thousand badly trained and poorly officered militia. The city was easily taken and the Capitol, the Congressional Library, President's house (the occupant had fled), and executive offices ruthlessly burned. Baltimore was more stoutly defended, and the bombardment brought forth Francis Scott Key's "Star-Spangled Banner." If the naval blockade showed the futility of a tiny navy, however efficient, the sack of Washington showed the incompetence of a poorly trained militia. Madison had to withstand a storm of indignation.

ANDREW JACKSON AT THE BATTLE OF NEW ORLEANS

Andrew Jackson was the hero of the defense of New Orleans in 1815. His tremendous energy and great common sense made him a successful soldier and President, for both of which careers he was untrained. The British were contemptuous of the American militia. They had reason for this. They made the mistake, however, of underestimating Jackson's ability. He drove them off, saved the mouth of the Mississippi, and restored the faith of the people in their fighting ability.

TREATY OF GHENT

Negotiations for peace began in 1814. Neither side gained by the terms. The searching of our ships and the impressment of our sailors, for which we had gone to war, were not even mentioned. The Canadian border was left for adjustment by a commission. The treaty was signed the day before Christmas, 1814. When Jackson's men ceased firing at New Orleans on the following January 8th, a peace that has lasted ever since began between the two English-speaking nations.

WAR WITH TRIPOLI: DECATUR'S EXPLOIT

A war with Tripoli was brought on in 1801 by the practise of the Barbary states of demanding "presents" (tribute) for the privilege of trading in the Mediterranean. Our navy gained valuable fighting experience in the war and acquitted itself with honor. Tripoli eventually gave up her demands. An outstanding act of bravery in the war was Stephen Decatur's entrance in 1804 on a ketch into the harbor of Tripoli, and the firing of a captive American ship.

BATTLE OF TIPPECANOE

Under a treaty made in 1809, which some of the Indians, including Tecumseh and his brother The Prophet, denounced as illegal, the whites began moving in large numbers into Indiana. Tecumseh raised the tribes in opposition. Some of them surprised William Henry Harrison at Tippecanoe in 1811 but were forced to retreat by his overwhelming force. The trouble was a prelude to 1812, for the Indians had been aided by Canada. Harrison was undeservedly hailed as a great conqueror.

FROM THE PAINTING BY ALONZO CHAPPEL.

THE BLACK HAWK WAR: BATTLE OF BAD AXE

Tecumseh in 1811 had had some chance of success, but Black Hawk in
1831, not appreciating that the day of the Indian in the old northwest was
over, had none. His pathetic attempt to win back his lands on the eastern
bank of the Mississippi, from which he had been dispossessed, stirs the
admiration. He was defeated with ruthless slaughter at Bad Axe in 1832,
and he was himself taken prisoner and paraded through the streets of our
cities like a circus animal.

197

THE SEMINOLE WAR: OSCEOLA

When in 1833–1835 it was proposed to remove the Indian inhabitants from Florida, the Seminoles under a gallant half-breed leader rose in revolt. By his ability to escape to swamps when closely pressed, Osceola spread terror and death throughout the country and always escaped capture. Eventually he was treacherously seized under a flag of truce, but the war dragged on until 1842 when the remnants of his warriors consented to be shipped away.

THE TEXAN REVOLT: FALL OF THE ALAMO

The American inhabitants of Texas rose to a man in 1836 when Mexico showed an intent to limit their political rights. At the old fort of the Alamo a small band of less than two hundred was surrounded by Santa Anna. The defenders held out for thirteen days (some say eleven), when, all but a handful being dead, the place was taken by storm. News of the heroic defense and murder of the six survivors roused the memorable cry, "Remember the Alamo." Uniting under Sam Houston, the Texans, helped by sympathetic volunteers from the states, lured Santa Anna far northward to his destruction at San Jacinto in April. The American continent has not witnessed braver fighting than in the Texan revolt.

BATTLE OF BUENA VISTA

The Mexican War began in 1846 as a result of the annexation of Texas.
General Zachary Taylor moved first into northern Mexico. He gained the
strongly fortified town of Monterey and then, although handicapped by the
fact that half of his army had been sent to Vera Cruz, won the battle of
Buena Vista on February 22–23, 1847, completely defeating Santa Anna.
He became the hero of his country and the following year was elected
President.

THE CALIFORNIA EXPEDITION: FRÉMONT RAISES THE EMBLEM OF THE BEAR FLAG REPUBLIC

The second offensive movement in the war was planned against California. Colonel Stephen W. Kearney was directed to march overland to that territory, with the object of taking and holding the land now embraced by New Mexico, Arizona, and California. He had gone as far as Santa Fé when the guide, Kit Carson, brought him news of events on the coast. John C. Frémont, an army officer engaged in a supposedly peaceful tour of exploration in California, had lent himself to the movement known as the Bear Flag Republic. He figured in the military activities which that move for freedom from Mexico brought on, until he was sent back to the United States for court martial. His course in California's break from Mexico has ever since been subject to varying interpretations. By the time Kearney arrived, Mexico's influence in California's affairs was not large.

THE MEXICANS EVACUATING VERA CRUZ

The war was not won by the victories in California nor in northern Mexico but by Winfield Scott's brilliant march to Mexico City. He secured the surrender of Vera Cruz, then by fierce attacks took the strong positions of Cerro Gordo, Molino del Rey, and Chapultepec. On September 13, 1847, he stood before Mexico City. The next day the capital surrendered. The war was won. Despite some feeling that we should demand all of Mexico we settled on approximately the present boundary, which gave us New Mexico and California.

LIBERTY. THE FAIR MAID OF KANSAS—IN THE HANDS OF THE "BORDER RUFFIANS"

COURTESY NEW YORK HISTORICAL SOCIETY.

THE KANSAS–NEBRASKA ACT

When in 1854 it was proposed to make a territory out of the Nebraska country, the nation again realized that the slavery issue was not dead. It was only sleeping. Stephen A. Douglas now secured the passage of the famous Kansas-Nebraska Act with its doctrine of "popular sovereignty" (sometimes called "squatter sovereignty"), i.e., the people of each territory, when making their state constitution, are to decide whether it be free or slave. The Act repealed the Missouri Compromise, and was the first link in a chain of events which led to the Civil War.

203

AN ILLUSTRATION FROM "UNCLE TOM'S CABIN": LITTLE
EVA READING THE BIBLE TO UNCLE TOM

In the campaign of 1856 the book *Uncle Tom's Cabin*, by Harriet Beecher
Stowe, played an important part in making Buchanan's margin of victory
a narrow one. His opponent was Fremont of California fame, the first
Presidential candidate of the Republicans. The book was an impassioned
protest against the fugitive slave law and although it overdrew the misery
of the slave, thousands in the North put it down with the conviction that
something should be done to remedy an inhuman situation. The book
helped prepare the North, psychologically, for war.

DRED SCOTT DECISION: CHIEF JUSTICE TANEY

The Dred Scott decision of the Supreme Court in 1857 showed the North that a peaceful solution of the slavery question was not to be had by judicial decision. In this momentous case the court, of which Roger B. Taney was Chief Justice, held that not only was a slave property but that the Missouri Compromise was unconstitutional, and no Negro could plead in a United States court as a citizen. It was a complete rebuff for the anti-slavery party. Scott, a Negro, based his plea for freedom on the claim that a two-year residence in free territory made him free. Following the decision Northern aid and assistance to fugitive slaves became more and more widespread and open.

THE LINCOLN–DOUGLAS DEBATES

The debates that Lincoln and Douglas held throughout Illinois in the contest for the senatorship in 1858 showed the country clearly something that it vaguely sensed but which it hesitated to put into words. Lincoln had put it into memorable words in June, 1858, before the convention which nominated him for the senatorship: "A house divided against itself cannot stand . . . it will become all one thing or all the other." By this extreme statement which he knew was true and which he dared state openly for the first time he lost the senatorship but won the presidency, for he convinced the North. The most important question in the debates themselves was expressed when Lincoln asked Douglas, "Can the people of a United States territory in any lawful way, against the wish of any citizen of the United States, exclude slavery from its limits prior to the formation of a State Constitution?" If Douglas had answered, "No," he might not have been elected senator. He chose to answer, "Yes," and thereby greatly increased the difficulty in his nomination by the Democratic Party in 1860, because the answer revealed to the South the fallaciousness of Douglas's doctrine of popular sovereignty. Thus was forged another link in the chain leading to war.

JOHN BROWN'S RAID: BROWN LED OUT FOR EXECUTION

John Brown's raid on Harper's Ferry, Virginia, in 1859, caused a shudder to run through the South. Brown was an irresponsible fanatic but his attempt to raise the slaves and arm them against their masters had enormous consequences. During Brown's trial and execution he bore himself with remarkable fortitude and so became a hero in Northern eyes. The South was now convinced that many in the North were determined not only to deprive them of their property but to do it by arming their human property.

JEFFERSON DAVIS INAUGURATED

The chain of events which began with the Kansas-Nebraska Act reached its end when Abraham Lincoln was elected President in 1860. The radical secessionists in the South, who had split the Democratic party and nominated Breckinridge, while the conservatives nominated Douglas, realized that the time had come, and justified themselves by reason of the election of the President by a party unnecessarily sectional. It was now or never. In February, 1861, South Carolina, Georgia, Alabama, Mississippi, Louisiana, and Florida (Texas, Arkansas, Tennessee, North Carolina, and Virginia later followed) met at Montgomery, Alabama, and established the Confederate States of America. On February 18th, Jefferson Davis became President.

ABRAHAM LINCOLN INAUGURATED

Between election day in 1860 and inaugural the following March, the nation held its breath, waiting. Would Lincoln save the Union or let the Southern states secede? The tall man from Illinois, on whom all eyes were turned, slipped secretly into Washington to take the oath of office and deliver his inaugural address. It held the answer to the fatal question. Kindly, he stated he would defend the Union and preserve the Constitution he had just sworn to support. But it was too late to do this peaceably.

FROM "FRANK LESLIE'S ILLUSTRATED NEWSPAPER" FOR MARCH 16, 1861.

BOMBARDMENT OF FORT SUMTER

Even now each side hesitated to strike the first blow. But it was soon to
come. When Lincoln ordered ships to go to the relief of Fort Sumter, within
the boundary of the Confederacy, the Southern agents who were in Washington arranging for the fort's surrender and for recognition, went home.
On April 12th the order to fire on the fort and its federal flag was given.
After a thirty-four-hour bombardment Sumter surrendered. War had begun.

STONEWALL JACKSON AT THE BATTLE OF BULL RUN

The cry in the North soon became "On to Richmond." It was a fine idea but one not to be realized for four bloody years. At Bull Run near Washington, on July 21, 1861, the raw Union troops were checked in their rash advance. Here Thomas J. Jackson won his nickname, "Stonewall." The Northern retreat became a rout when the troops tangled with the carriages of congressmen and their wives who had driven out from the Capitol to see the great victory.

FROM A PAINTING BY H. A. OGDEN.   COPYRIGHT, 1900, JONES BROS. PUBLISHING CO

THE "TRENT" AFFAIR: THE "SAN JACINTO" STOPS THE "TRENT"

FROM "THE ILLUSTRATED LONDON NEWS" FOR DECEMBER 7, 1861.

Throughout the war the South strove to win English recognition for the Confederacy. It never came and its failure contributed to defeat. The mass of the English people were unsympathetic to slavery and this, basically, decided the issue. In 1861, however, England and the North came near blows when the American ship San Jacinto seized on the high seas the British ship Trent on which were Mason and Slidell, two Confederate emissaries journeying to Europe.

BATTLE OF SHILOH

In the early days of the war the Southern troops had the advantage. Both Davis and his military adviser, Robert E. Lee, were West Pointers. Lincoln knew nothing of military art. The South recognized the ability of the Southern aristocracy to command and its troops obeyed them willingly, making good soldiers; while the untrained men of the Northern cities brought a spirit of independence into the trenches ill-suited to military discipline. The North, however, had the advantage of numbers, wealth, and natural resources. These factors, in the end, turned the tide. It must be remembered that the Confederate leaders never thought of capturing or conquering the North. They hoped, at best, to prevent the North from accomplishing the far more difficult task of conquering them, and they nearly accomplished their purpose. The military history of the war divides simply into two parts, a western and an eastern campaign. The object of the first was to win the Mississippi Valley, and then strike at the heart of the Confederacy from the west. The first great battle in the war was at Shiloh, on April 6th and 7th, 1862. It was also the opening gun of the western campaign. Ulysses S. Grant won his first major success, pushing the enemy back to Corinth in Mississippi.

213

FALL OF VICKSBURG

The Confederacy now lost Memphis and New Orleans. Vicksburg was the
one strong point left them on the river. If it fell, Texas, Arkansas, and
Louisiana would be cut off from the Confederacy. Grant now came south
from Tennessee and by fine generalship cut off Vicksburg and began a
siege which ended, after stubborn resistance, on July 4, 1863. The day before, the Battle of Gettysburg had been won in the eastern campaign.
The North was jubilant.

BATTLE OF MISSIONARY RIDGE

General William Rosecrans, having won the Battle of Chickamauga in September, occupied Chattanooga and awaited Grant's arrival. The Confederates, under Braxton Bragg, occupied the heights of Lookout Mountain and Missionary Ridge outside the city. On November 24th and 25th the energetic Grant gave battle. William T. Sherman pushed back one wing, while Joseph Hooker took the mountain. Then George H. Thomas's troops, against orders, charged the center of the ridge, taking the crest. All of Tennessee had now been captured, and Atlanta was threatened.

SIEGE OF ATLANTA

Grant now became commander-in-chief, leaving Sherman in charge of the west. By a series of clever flanking movements executed through the summer of 1864, Sherman forced Joseph E. Johnston and then J. B. Hood back on Atlanta, which was evacuated in September. When he later began his march to the sea, Georgia "howled," as he said it would. This march split the Confederacy, but the same end might have been accomplished without the destruction he spread in his wake.

SHERMAN'S SOLDIERS FORAGING DURING THE MARCH TO THE SEA

Sherman dealt the South a blow which it was never to forget. He reached the seacoast at Savannah in middle December. In February, 1865, he turned north, spreading even worse destruction than in Georgia. His object was to join Grant against Richmond, but he was not needed there. The job of the western army was over. With inferior forces the Confederacy had contested every foot of its advance, only laying down its arms when exhausted by overwhelming forces.

217

FROM "HARPER'S WEEKLY" FOR JULY 26, 1862.

FIGHTING AT MALVERN HILL DURING THE SEVEN DAYS' BATTLE OF THE RICHMOND CAMPAIGN

The story of the eastern campaign is far different from that in the west. The North tasted defeat frequently, and once the cause of union came near destruction. It was marked by one futile attempt after another to find a competent general, a problem that was not solved until Grant's ascendancy in 1864. The first major move after Bull Run was again against Richmond, a campaign which George B. McClellan commanded and which culminated in the Seven Days' Battle, June 26 to July 1, 1862. The campaign failed, not because some battles were not won but because Joseph E. Johnston and Robert E. Lee halted, in the end, this attempt to take Richmond from the coast side.

218

BATTLE OF ANTIETAM

In late August at the second battle of Bull Run the Confederates, under the able generals Lee, Jackson, and James Longstreet, inflicted a crushing defeat on John Pope, the new commander. Lee then struck into Maryland. McClellan, replacing Pope, met him at Antietam, on September 17, 1862, in the bloodiest day of the war. Lee lost 11,000, McClellan 12,400. It was a Union victory and Lee recrossed the Potomac, but McClellan, failing to pursue him diligently, lost his command.

THE PROCLAMATION OF EMANCIPATION

Lincoln waited for a victory to proclaim the slaves in the rebel states free. Antietam in September, 1862, gave him his opportunity. Emancipation was proclaimed soon after, to become effective January 1, at which time a final proclamation was put forth. From this were omitted Tennessee and parts of other states, where the Union forces held control. The South did not observe it, but from then on, in addition to preservation of the Union, the war was waged for the abolition of slavery. The Thirteenth Amendment, constitutionally abolishing slavery, was ratified in 1865, and the conquered states accepted it after the war.

220

BATTLE OF CHANCELLORSVILLE

General A. E. Burnside now became commander of the Army of the Potomac. On December 13, 1862, in another attempt on Richmond, he lost the battle of Fredericksburg. The North was in despair. The energetic Hooker now replaced Burnside. He met Lee and Jackson at Chancellorsville on May 2 to 4, 1863. It was the last great Confederate victory. The three days' fighting lost both sides a total of 30,000 men. Stonewall Jackson fell, shot by mistake by his own sentinels.

FROM A PAINTING BY H. A. OGDEN.   COPYRIGHT, 1900, JONES BROS. PUBLISHING CO.

JEB STUART'S RAID

Lee now decided to invade Union territory, hoping that a victory would induce the North to make peace. He started in early June, 1863, and so adroit was the work of his cavalry under J. E. B. Stuart that it was days before Hooker perceived what was afoot. Stuart now made one of the raids for which he was noted but which was, on this occasion, disastrous. He dashed behind the Federals, reached Carlisle, Pennsylvania, only to arrive at Gettysburg with exhausted men and horses.

BATTLE OF GETTYSBURG

The Union forces, now commanded by George Gordon Meade, followed Lee north. In Gettysburg, Pennsylvania, on July 1, the advance divisions of both armies met and joined battle. The day ended with a Union retreat, with the Confederates on Seminary Ridge, and their opponents frantically digging in on the rise of ground opposite, made by Culp's Hill, Cemetery Hill, Little Round Top, and Big Round Top. The fighting on the 2nd pushed both of Meade's flanks back. He assumed, rightly, that next day the attack would come on the center. George E. Pickett's division led that attack on the afternoon of the 3rd. Standing in front of Seminary Ridge, a mile from his objective, he began the advance. For a quarter of a mile he was protected, the rest was open ground. Across it came the grey lines, wave on wave, meeting and passing through a murderous fire. At last the Union lines were gained. For some few minutes the outcome was in doubt, then Pickett's men wavered. Back across the open space they went. The high tide of the Confederate arms left its mark on Cemetery Hill. Lee retreated to Virginia.

LINCOLN'S GETTYSBURG ADDRESS

FROM "HARPER'S WEEKLY," FEBRUARY 10, 1900.

Four months passed and the President came on November 19th to Gettysburg to dedicate the cemetery where lay buried men of both sides. In one brief page of remarkable prose Lincoln spoke his philosophy. ". . . that we here highly resolve that these dead shall not have died in vain, that this nation under God shall have a new birth of freedom, and that Government of the people, by the people, for the people, shall not perish from the earth."

224

BATTLE OF THE WILDERNESS: ATTACK AT SPOTTSYLVANIA

Both armies rested after Gettysburg. Grant became commander in March, 1864. His campaign was designed to crush Lee by sheer numbers. He fought the drawn Battle of The Wilderness in early May, then flanked and met Lee again at Spottsylvania Court House from May 8th to 21st. Again he was checked, but he wrote back, "I propose to fight it out on this line if it takes all summer." Again and again he flanked, losing some battles, winning no conclusive ones, but forcing Lee back to Richmond, to which he laid siege.

LEE RIDING TO APPOMATTOX COURT HOUSE

In early April the doomed city of Richmond fell, but Lee fled west. Grant followed. The end came on April 9, 1865, at Appomattox Court House. Even the brave Lee could hold out no longer. When the two great generals met to decide the terms of surrender, Grant won Lee's affection by allowing him and his officers to keep their side-arms, and his troops their horses. Said Lee, "It will be very gratifying and do much toward conciliating our people." Had Grant's generosity and Lincoln's magnanimity been displayed by those soon to direct the nation, the sad story of the reconstruction years would not have been.

BLOCKADE OF THE SOUTH: THE "MONITOR" AND THE "MERRIMAC"

The most important naval part of the war was the blockade of the southern coast. The Confederates, in 1862, constructed the iron-clad *Virginia* (earlier, the *Merrimac*), in an effort to break the blockade. On March 9, 1862, having had one day of glorious destruction, she met the *Monitor*, "a raft with a cheese-box on it." The battle was fierce and the *Virginia* retired. It marked the end of the hey-day of the wooden war ship.

CAPTURE OF NEW ORLEANS: BOMBARDING THE FORTS BELOW THE CITY

While the Union forces were recuperating after Shiloh, David G. Farragut undertook to capture New Orleans by water. It was a brilliant but dangerous plan, for the approach to the great Southern city was guarded by two strong forts. After five days of bombarding the forts Farragut decided to run between them. Early in the morning of April 24, 1862, he started. Once his flagship, the *Hartford*, went aground and was dangerously near destruction. Eventually his fleet passed through the heavy cross-fire from the forts. Once past them, the forts were cut off from assistance and surrendered. New Orleans surrendered soon after. The victory had profound moral effects in both North and South, and also on feeling toward the South in Europe, where the city was well known, especially to the French.

RAIDERS: THE "KEARSARGE" AND THE "ALABAMA"

Some ships escaped the blockade. Most famous of these was the Confederate raider *Alabama* under Raphael Semmes. She took, in all, thirty-six vessels. At last, at Cherbourg, France, on June 19, 1864, she was cornered by the *Kearsarge*, but bravely gave battle to her more heavily armed opponent. Not only was the *Kearsarge* heavier but she carried cleverly concealed chain mantlets protecting her engine room. Round and round the two ships fought, starboard to starboard. Finally the *Alabama* struck, then plunged downward, stern first.

FARRAGUT ON THE "HARTFORD" AT MOBILE BAY

Farragut was the outstanding naval commander of the North. On August 5, 1864, he won his great victory at Mobile Bay. Passing the forts commanding the harbor, he concentrated on the powerful ram *Tennessee*. Shot from ship after ship struck her armored sides without effect. Finally, her steering gear disabled, she surrendered. The victory put an end to blockade-running in this section and cheered the North, which was then reading the death lists of Grant's campaigns in Virginia.

LINCOLN AS PRESIDENT

From first to last, Lincoln's aim was to preserve the Union. That idea dictated his policy, military and political. As the war progressed he led the country as no other man has ever done. His character, in which honesty and sincerity prevailed, enabled him to do this. In March, 1865, he assumed office for the second time, and with it the problems of reconstruction. It is to him that today we owe a unified nation. The photographs show how his face changed in the four years between his first and second inaugural.

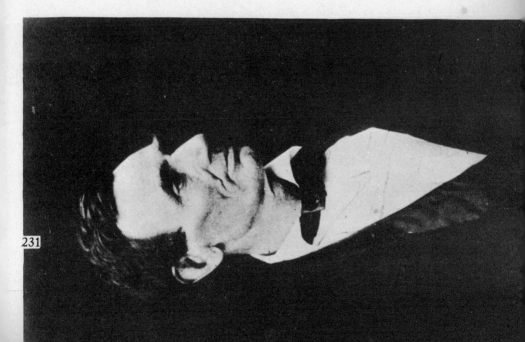

ASSASSINATION OF LINCOLN

Said Lincoln on April 14th: "I hope that there will be no persecution, no
bloody work after the war is over." That night, in Ford's Theater, Washington, demented John Wilkes Booth shot him through the head. Booth
leaped from the Presidential box to the stage, breaking his leg. That he
then turned, shouting "*Sic semper tyrannis*," is probably untrue. Booth
was killed on April 26, while trying to escape, and his co-conspirators
hanged, but that did not remedy the terrible blow his bullet had dealt the
nation, especially the South.

RIOTING DURING RECONSTRUCTION DAYS IN NEW ORLEANS

People differed violently as to how the South should be brought back into the Union and the Negro given civil status. President Andrew Johnson was for a moderate policy, involving the minimum of humiliation. But the radicals in Congress, under Thaddeus Stevens, soon overpowered him, set up military governments in the South, and insisted that the Negro have all the civil rights of white men. Violence was inevitable. The controversy proved again that the habits of generations cannot be changed by legislative act.

FROM "HARPER'S WEEKLY" FOR AUGUST 25, 1866.

ECONOMIC RUIN OF THE SOUTH: FEEDING THE POOR

The war left the South prostrate. Every business and banking institution that had done business with the government was bankrupt or nearly so. Soldiers returned to barren fields or to bread lines in the cities. To all these woes were added the acts of the radicals in Washington. The whites soon came to believe that nothing more except death could happen. So grew up the "Solid South," dominated by a deep-bred resentment against any political policy labeled "Republican."

FEEDING THE POOR AT NEW ORLEANS.

"CARPET-BAGGERS," "SCALAWAGS," AND A SOUTHERN LEGISLATURE

The end of the war brought an influx of poor Northerners to the South. They came carrying in carpet-bags all their possessions. Hence the term of derision. Many of the Negroes, who had suddenly gained the vote by reason of the hasty passage of the Fourteenth and Fifteenth amendments, fell easily under the influence of the worst "carpet-baggers," and the ensuing corruption, especially in the legislatures, was worse than anything the country experienced before or since. The "scalawags" were poor whites who saw in reconstruction a chance to better themselves and began to run for political office on the Republican ticket.

235

Plan of the Contemplated Murder of John Campbell.

(Entered according to Act of Congress, September, 1871, by T. B. Stampft.)

The scene which furnishes the subject of the above engraving, was witnessed at a place known as Big Poplar, Moore county, North Carolina, on the night of the 10th of August. A man named John Campbell, a worthy resident of that locality, had, by his strict and earnest devotion to the cause of the Republican party, placed himself under the ban of the "White Brotherhood." He had been adjudged guilty at one of their many secret meetings of this, in their opinion, crime, and sentenced to be hung. Of course, the victim was unconscious of the fate in store for him, and was quietly resting in his home when the murderous band of Ku-Klux, who had been charged with the duty of dispatching him, surrounded the house, captured their inoffensive and unsuspecting prey, secured his own wagon, then in solemn procession marched to an adjoining wood where the hellish deed was to be consummated. But an agent for their destruction was there, of which they little dreamed. Under one of the disguises strode the stalwart figure of a faithful agent of the Government, in the per-

son of Captain Joseph G. Hester, one of the oft-tried employees of the United States secret service. He had his arrangements made, as will be subsequently shown in the article, and unless some unforeseen accident occurred the captive then being led to his death would soon be free.

Arrived at the wood Campbell was taken from the wagon, and a half circle formed of the murderous brotherhood; the rope was produced, the hangman's noose placed over the head of the intended martyr, who, trembling with fear, was made to kneel before the assassinating band, thirsting for his blood, while the dread sentence of death was pronounced upon him. This scene of terror is faithfully depicted by our artist. With cowled head the Ku-Klux stand, their hands grasping the cord with which they expected soon to swing their victim into eternity. The sentence was pronounced, a movement was made to proceed with the execution, when suddenly Hester gave the signal he had previously arranged. Instantly the fiendish gang were surrounded with armed men, the rope

snatched from the neck of the liberated captive, the disguises stripped from his captors, strong hands seized theirs, and the timely handcuff made to perform its functions.

The prisoners were marched to Raleigh, where Capt. Hester, with a desire that the people at large may know, without actual inspection, what a Ku Klux tribunal looks like, formed the group as it was formed in the woods, photographed it, and from the copy forwarded by him to the Secretary of War we have caused to be made a faithful fac simile in wood, which is presented to our readers. The names of some of the party engaged in this operation are as follows: Wm. W. Wicker, Jesse Bryan, J. W. Gaster, Wm. J. Bryan, R. W. Bryan and D. McIver, all of Moore county.

Bryan and Wicker, who are charged with the murder of Murchison McLane, were committed to jail to await an examination which is postponed two weeks for want of witness. The other four were allowed to give bail in the sum of $2,000 each for their appearance

at the September term of the United States Circuit Court.

John Gaster turned State's evidence, and his developments will reveal a state of affairs which will startle the public, and implicate parties little suspected.

Of course Hester's part in the capture narrated could not be kept secret, and the Democratic press in some portions of the State opened up against them vials of wrath. We quote from the Fayetteville Eagle the manner in which the editor proposes to get clear of this faithful ally of the Government:

"Hester and other suspicious characters are prowling around in the country as secret detectives, really secret agents of the Radical officials, to keep up political hate and strife for profit to that party and its leaders. We hope our citizens will shoot down, on sight, any strangers caught in mischief while sneaking stealthily about our houses. A legitimate and well-meaning Government employee should be respected and assisted; but an assassin and incendiary, and a base tool for low-lived treachery and oppression, should not be allowed to carry out his nefarious purposes."

THE KU KLUX KLAN

Reconstruction as dictated by Congress led to inevitable violence. The South, determined to keep the freedmen peaceable and their white leaders in check, organized the Ku Klux Klan. First, its members resorted only to ghostly visits, then came whippings, tar, and feathers, and finally death. In 1871 Congress gave the President the right to suppress the organization, and the South, having had enough of violence, disbanded it. From a practical point of view, it had served its purpose.

Conflict between the President and the radicals over reconstruction policies at last reached such a state that the Senate made an attempt to impeach him. He was uncouth, at least on one occasion under the influence of liquor, and rash in his statements. These, however, were not crimes. As the trial progressed, the nation and some few in Congress relented. On May 16, 1867, the vote was taken in breathless anticipation. Johnson held his office by one vote. The radicals were defeated. The country returned to sanity.

FROM "FRANK LESLIE'S ILLUSTRATED NEWSPAPER" FOR SEPTEMBER 3, 1864.

MAXIMILIAN'S RECEPTION AT MEXICO CITY

Ferdinand Maximilian's attempt to establish himself as emperor of Mexico was halted in 1865 when, the coming of peace having left the United States with a large army still mobilized, the federal government demanded that the French troops, which had subdued Mexico from 1861 on, be withdrawn. Napoleon acceded, but Maximilian stuck to his post. Surrounded by corruption he was betrayed at Querétaro, in 1867, captured by the Mexicans and, despite our pleas and those of others, shot.

PURCHASE OF ALASKA: NEW ARCHANGEL IN 1867

In both the Maximilian affair and the securing of Alaska in 1867, Seward, Johnson's Secretary of State, showed himself adept at foreign affairs. Alaska's fur trade and fishing industry were valuable, but Russia found it too remote to govern well, and fearing it might be seized by England, asked whether the United States was interested in purchasing the territory. The suggestion was quickly accepted. In one evening a price of $7,000,000 was agreed on, and a treaty drawn before either of the parties had a chance to change their minds. In the text accompanying the above illustration in *Harper's Weekly*, the editors of that magazine were skeptical of the bargain that had been made. Admitting that the new possessions were large, they said, "their value is another question."

FROM "HARPER'S WEEKLY" FOR MAY 4, 1867.

239

BUILDING THE TRANSCONTINENTAL RAILROAD: DRIVING
THE GOLDEN SPIKE

The linking of East and West by rail was the climax of one of the most colorful stories of American commercial enterprise. Although planned before the Civil War, the transcontinental railroad was not completed till several years afterward. Aided by government funds, the Union Pacific built westward and the Central Pacific eastward. The frantic race between the two was for the valuable land grants, as well as the subsidies, that went with each mile of new track. At Promontory Point, Utah, on May 10, 1869, a golden spike was driven into the last tie. The Central Pacific was said to have won by a small margin.

240

THE NEW YORK STOCK EXCHANGE ON "BLACK FRIDAY"

The panic of September 24, 1869, came as the result of an attempt by Jay Gould and James Fisk, Jr., to corner the country's gold supply. Gould had wormed his way into the good graces of President Grant and made him an unwitting partner to the manipulation. Gold rose from 132 to 162. During the price rise Gould sold not only to the public but to Fisk. When the government broke the corner by selling gold, Gould was safely out of the market with a handsome profit, Fisk was ruined, and Grant discredited.

THE CHICAGO FIRE

The great Chicago fire began on October 8, 1871. The conflagration, said to have started in a stable where a cow kicked over a lighted lamp, burned for three days, in some places reached the edge of the prairie itself, consumed three and a half square miles of city buildings, snuffed out two hundred and fifty lives, and caused a loss of about $200,000,000. It was not without its benefits to the future citizens of Chicago, however, for the people of the city rapidly rebuilt it along finer and more splendid lines.

242

THE GREAT TIDE OF IMMIGRATION: EMBARKATION FOR NEW YORK

A great period of prosperity was attained throughout the country, except in the ruined South, from 1865 to 1873. The railroad projects, followed by agricultural expansion in the West, and many new enterprises which were now beginning, created a demand for cheap labor. It was supplied from abroad. Hundreds of thousands of immigrants were soon swarming into our ports, many of them being unsuited to life in the new country. This was the beginning of the long period in which the United States became the "melting pot" of the world.

FROM "HARPER'S WEEKLY" FOR OCTOBER 11, 1873.

PANIC OF 1873: OFFICES OF JAY COOKE & CO.

Over-expansion brought its consequences in September, 1873. The banking firm of Jay Cooke & Co. had financed the building of the Northern Pacific. At about the same time there was a sharp panic in Vienna, Austria, and Europe, alarmed, ceased buying American bonds. Gradually it became apparent that Cooke could not market the Northern Pacific securities. The firm's admission of insolvency on the 18th started a bank run, and this uncertainty eventually spreading to the entire business structure of the nation, began a long period of "hard times."

RISE OF THE TEMPERANCE CRUSADE

A temperance movement grew rapidly in the 1870's and 1880's. Although
there had been agitation against strong drink for years, it was not till 1874
that the National Woman's Christian Temperance Union was founded.
Frances Willard became the moving spirit in the organization. Although
this picture shows the temperance advocates in a pacific mood, on many
occasions destruction of all movable furnishings marked their visits to a
saloon.

FROM "THE DAILY GRAPHIC" FOR MARCH 5, 1874.

245

THE BELKNAP SCANDAL AND GRANT'S POLITICAL MISTAKES

Although honest himself, Grant had an easy toleration of corruption in others, and his two terms marked the heyday of the spoilsman. Following the Gould-Fisk speculation came the Credit Mobilier frauds, the Whisky Ring, and the Belknap scandal in 1876, in which it was said that Belknap, Grant's Secretary of War, accepted a bribe to keep an Indian agent in office. It was inevitable that the corrupt and often illicit, but very profitable, trade with the Indians in the West should bring corruption to high places. With none of these scandals was Grant directly involved, but his friends and advisers were, and his reputation suffered accordingly.

FROM A CARTOON BY THOMAS NAST IN "HARPER'S WEEKLY" FOR MARCH 25, 1876.

246

FROM "FRANK LESLIE'S ILLUSTRATED NEWSPAPER" FOR DECEMBER 2, 1876.

THE DISPUTED ELECTION OF 1876: THE COMMISSION IN SESSION

The Presidential election of 1876 resulted in a political dispute of serious proportions. Rutherford B. Hayes, Republican, had 184 undisputed votes, Samuel J. Tilden, Democrat, 165, with twenty from South Carolina, Louisiana, Florida, and Oregon, in dispute. Tilden needed them all to be elected. Eventually an electoral commission of fifteen men was appointed by Congress to decide the issue. On this there were eight Republicans and seven Democrats. Its decision was along strictly party lines, and Hayes became President.

CUSTER MASSACRE: CUSTER RAIDS AN INDIAN CAMP

The Sioux War of 1876 was the last serious attempt of the Indian to hold by arms some of the land to which he had been born. Joining with the Cheyennes, the Sioux, under their able leader Sitting Bull, raised a powerful force of some six thousand braves. In late June they trapped General G.A. Custer and six hundred men near the junction of the Big Horn and the Little Big Horn rivers in South Dakota. Not a soldier in Custer's party escaped. The slaughter was probably as ruthless as the Army's methods had been in attacking Indian villages.

248

THE CENTENNIAL EXPOSITION: OPENING DAY

The Centennial Exposition held in Philadelphia in 1876 celebrated the one hundredth anniversary of American independence. It was the world's outstanding affair of that character held up to that time. Its educational and cultural advantages were great, for foreign and domestic contacts were then vastly less than today. Every important foreign country participated and Americans were thrown into touch with old-world products and culture as never before. Directly and indirectly, it had a material influence on international trade.

FROM "HARPER'S WEEKLY" FOR MAY 27, 1876.

THE CORLISS STEAM ENGINE AT THE CENTENNIAL

One of the high spots of the Exposition was the starting of the great Corliss steam engine, the wonder of the day, which turned the machinery in Machinery Hall. Dom Pedro, the emperor of Brazil, accompanied by President Grant, turned on the power which put the huge machine in motion. It was purchased by the Pullman Company following the close of the Exposition and for many years ran in its plant at Chicago.

BELL DEMONSTRATES THE TELEPHONE AT SALEM

Included in an educational exhibit from Massachusetts at the Centennial Exposition was a device destined to revolutionize sound transmission. It had been sent there by a young Scotsman named Alexander Graham Bell. It attracted little attention until, in the following year, a public exhibition of the "telephone" was given at Salem, Massachusetts. To the amazement of those present, a spoken message was successfully transmitted from that city to the office of a Boston newspaper.

FROM "FRANK LESLIE'S ILLUSTRATED NEWSPAPER" FOR MARCH 31, 1877.

THE ELECTRIC LIGHT

Many had experimented with electric lighting before Thomas A. Edison put in circuit the first commercially successful lamp on October 21, 1879. When the New York papers announced that Edison was lighting the streets of Menlo Park, New Jersey, with his new lamp, the Pennsylvania Railroad installed special trains to accommodate those who came to see the marvel. The picture shows New York, near the Fifth Avenue Hotel, when the city was illuminated by Brush arc lamps.

RIOTS AGAINST THE CHINESE, AND EXCLUSION

The presence of many Chinese in the Far West did not cause much opposition until white laborers, pouring in with the coming of the transcontinental railroads, complained because the Chinese worked long hours for little pay. Serious riots against them took place in many cities, such as the one shown below in Denver in 1880. Hayes finally negotiated a treaty with China which for ten years excluded Chinese laborers. Later, this treaty was extended indefinitely. It was always difficult to enforce, due to smuggling.

FROM "FRANK LESLIE'S ILLUSTRATED NEWSPAPER" FOR NOVEMBER 20, 1880.

253

FROM "FRANK LESLIE'S ILLUSTRATED NEWSPAPER" FOR JANUARY 8, 1881.

SPECIE PAYMENT AND THE PROSPEROUS YEARS

Specie payment was not resumed by the United States until 1879. The question then was, could it be maintained? Two fortuitous events made this possible, first, a general failure of European crops causing a demand for our farm supplies; second, the failure of the cotton crop in India. Both helped turn the balance of trade in our favor and our gold remained with us. The picture, showing a levee in New Orleans in 1881, was entitled "The Business Boom in the South," at the time of its publication. Prosperity was nation-wide in the years 1879 to 1881.

254

GARFIELD'S ASSASSINATION: TRIAL OF GUITEAU

On July 2, 1881, while on his way to attend the Commencement exercises at Williams College, James A. Garfield, who had been in office but four months, was approached in the Washington railway station by a disappointed office seeker named Charles J. Guiteau, who shot him. He died on September 19th. During those weeks in which he lay suffering, much of the political feeling against him, due to his countenancing of some of the practices of the spoilsmen, disappeared. Guiteau, who was an obscure Chicago lawyer of French-Canadian descent, was tried and convicted in Washington, where he was hanged on June 30, 1882.

FROM "FRANK LESLIE'S ILLUSTRATED NEWSPAPER" FOR DECEMBER 3, 1881.

255

THE OPENING OF THE BROOKLYN BRIDGE

One of the great engineering feats of the late 19th century was the building
of the Brooklyn Bridge. The success of the venture was, in large measure,
due to the Roebling brothers who made the gigantic cables that held up the
roadway. One of them died in the construction work. Some time after it
was opened in 1883 someone on the span suddenly shouted that it was
falling and several persons were killed in the wild panic that followed.

256

CIVIL SERVICE REFORM

The period from 1881 to 1893 was marked by political and economic reform. One of the first things accomplished was the Civil Service Act of 1883. At last, in the face of an overwhelming public feeling against the spoils system, Congress gave way. Since 1883 successive Presidents have perfected and enlarged the system. Under Harrison, Theodore Roosevelt made the service a powerful agent for good. Congress feared him, the spoilsmen hated him, but the people trusted his judgment. The picture, "The Franking Abuse," shows bags of free mail leaving Washington. The Post Office was the prey for the spoilsmen and was soon affected for the better by the Civil Service reforms.

FROM A CARTOON IN "PUCK" BY F. OPPER.

257

"RUM, ROMANISM, AND REBELLION"

In 1884 the statement of one of James G. Blaine's admirers, a New York divine, to the effect that he and his friends would not vote for the party of "Rum, Romanism, and Rebellion," very likely caused his defeat. Blaine was at the reception when these words were spoken and in replying to the minister's speech, he took no notice of the slight to the Catholic church. The election hung on the outcome in New York which went Democratic by 1149 votes. With the result so close, it is probable that the statement turned the balance for Grover Cleveland, the Democratic candidate. The picture shows the reception at which the damaging statement was made.

THE HAYMARKET RIOTS

As the nation's industrial workers increased in numbers, organized labor under the banner of the Knights of Labor grew in power. Within the organization were many advocates of direct action and, at an anarchists' meeting in Haymarket Square, Chicago, in 1886, a bomb was thrown killing seven people. Eight anarchists were arrested. The country was vastly excited at this appearance of violence, and of the eight, four were hung, one committed suicide, and two received life sentences. The thrower of the bomb was never identified. People, generally, approved the sentences, although many have always maintained that the men were the victims of public hysteria and a prejudiced judge, and were given a trial that was irregular in many respects.

FROM "HARPER'S WEEKLY" FOR JULY 25, 1868.

FORMATION OF THE AMERICAN FEDERATION OF LABOR

The American Federation of Labor was organized under that name in 1886 while public reaction against the Knights was still strong. It held that workers in each trade should organize in their own interests, a system suited to the nature of American industry. Its growth was remarkable. Its earliest activities were devoted to securing shorter working hours. The picture shows New England mill workers in 1868 when twelve-hour shifts, employing women and children, were not uncommon. It was against such conditions that first the Knights and then the American Federation of Labor turned their efforts.

RAILROAD BUILDING AND CONSOLIDATION: A CHICAGO RAILWAY STATION

The period from 1850 on was first one of great railway construction, interrupted by the Civil War and the panics of 1857 and 1873, and then one of railway consolidation. In this era grew the nuclei of the New York Central, the Pennsylvania, and the Baltimore & Ohio systems. While consolidation went on, new tracks were being laid, especially in the west on the Central Pacific, the Union Pacific, the Northern Pacific, the Southern Pacific, the Santa Fé, and the Great Northern lines. From all this activity Chicago, as a junction point, benefited and its station platforms were the meeting points of the East and West.

CULVER SERVICE.

261

THE INTERSTATE COMMERCE COMMISSION ACT

Railroad consolidation brought evils in its wake. Public distrust of the roads led to the formation of the Granges in the West which, in their turn, hastened the coming of the first Interstate Commerce Commission Act in 1887. This act gave the commission no jurisdiction over rates and no power to enforce its decisions. Hence freight re-bates to favored shippers and discrimination against other shippers and shipping points went on as before, until after the turn of the century. The arm stretching from the White House, in the cartoon, is Cleveland's, under whose administration the I. C. C. Act was passed.

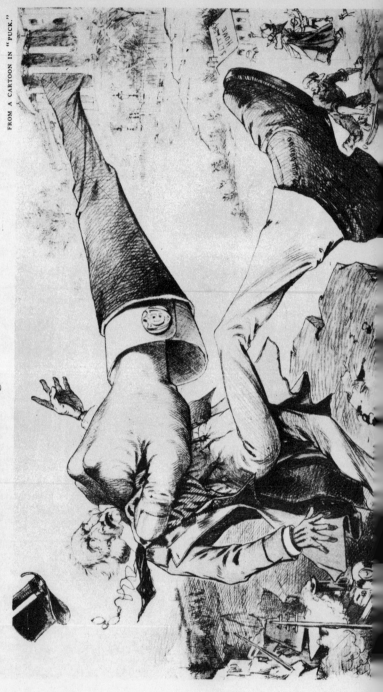

FROM A CARTOON IN "PUCK."

262

"HARPER'S WEEKLY" FOR JULY 27, 1889.

THE McKINLEY TARIFF: STEAMER DAY IN NEW YORK

A tariff was the first legislative act passed by the United States. That was in 1789. Ever since, protection has been a political battleground. The rise of American industry, and, to some degree, the need for revenue, spurred the tariff acts of the eighties and nineties. The McKinley Tariff of 1890 advanced rates somewhat. An attempt was made to embody in this bill the principle of reciprocity, but, as it was finally passed, it acted more as a club by which we were able to get trade concessions, especially from the South American countries. In 1894 the Wilson Bill brought reductions, but in 1897 the Dingley Bill raised the wall again. Capital and labor being in agreement on the subject of protection, this bill remained until 1909.

263

FROM "HARPER'S WEEKLY" FOR JUNE 15, 1889.

THE JOHNSTOWN FLOOD

Johnstown, Pennsylvania, was on May 31, 1889, the scene of one of the greatest disasters in American history. An abandoned reservoir, about twelve miles above the city, gave way and a huge mass of water tore down the valley of the Conemaugh River. The flood swept away the city and with it about three thousand lives. Some said that the flood was caused by excessive lumbering in the section which had denuded the surrounding hills, changing the natural drainage.

264

SHERMAN ANTI-TRUST ACT

This period was also one of great combinations in the industrial field. John D. Rockefeller first proved it possible to monopolize not only a public service but the manufacture of an article, with the formation of the Standard Oil Trust. Small business and the general public were instinctively against the trust and it became a political issue in 1888. In 1890 was passed the Sherman Anti-Trust Law. It declared illegal contracts to create monopolies in restraint of trade. It made no distinction between good and bad combinations, and later, changes became necessary in the anti-trust laws.

FROM A CARTOON BY W. A. ROGERS IN "HARPER'S WEEKLY" FOR DECEMBER 3, 1887.

FROM A CARTOON BY J. KEPPLER IN "PUCK" FOR FEBRUARY 6, 1889.

THE SAMOAN INCIDENT

The Samoan Islands in the Pacific became the subject of a controversy in 1889 among the United States, Great Britain, and Germany. War ships were anchored off the islands and a conflict seemed imminent when on March 16th a hurricane destroyed all but one of the vessels. A joint protectorate was then formed from which Great Britain later withdrew, the United States taking the island of Tutuila, and Germany the rest. During the incident there was hard feeling among the three nations, especially between the United States and Germany. In the World War, Germany lost her portion.

266

THE MAFIA INCIDENT: MURDER OF THE ITALIANS

On March 15, 1891, a mob in New Orleans broke open a prison where several Italians, suspected of being connected with the Mafia Society, a well-known Italian organization, and implicated in the murder of the city's chief of police, were detained. Nine were shot down. Washington could not grant the satisfaction Italy demanded because no federal law had been violated and Italy withdrew her representative. Most of the victims were American citizens and with this discovery Italy relented and an incident, for a moment dangerous, passed over.

FROM "HARPER'S WEEKLY" FOR MARCH 28, 1891.

FUR SEAL CONTROVERSY: SLAUGHTER OF THE SEALS

During President Harrison's administration the slaughter of the fur seals in Bering Sea was widely criticized. The United States claimed that its ownership of the Pribiloff Islands gave it the right to control sealing in the whole of the Bering Sea and proceeded to arrest persons taking seals contrary to its regulations. Great Britain vigorously protested. Public opinion in both countries was against violence and this forced a settlement in 1893. The two countries thereafter jointly regulated the industry.

THE HOMESTEAD STRIKE: SURRENDER OF THE PINKERTON MEN

Continuing industrial growth during the prosperous years after 1886 brought a corresponding increase in the power of organized labor which made possible the great strike at Homestead, Pennsylvania, in 1892, against the Carnegie Steel Company. In a battle between the workers and about two hundred detectives of the Pinkerton agency, seven were killed. Soldiers were called to keep order and the trouble died down. The conflict was won by the company and it was the last serious effort of the steel workers for a quarter of a century.

FROM "HARPER'S WEEKLY" FOR JULY 16, 1892.

THE PANIC OF 1893: THE STOCK EXCHANGE ON AUGUST 12

The panic of 1893 started when Europe began selling American securities and withdrawing gold. Our ability to maintain specie payment was threatened. Cleveland feared the public would begin hoarding gold. Business distress rapidly became widespread. When the Silver Purchase Law of 1890 was repealed in 1893, the West and the South felt that they had been betrayed by Cleveland. The gold-silver controversy now became more bitter than ever. The picture illustrates one of the flurries on the Stock Exchange during the panic.

270

THE PULLMAN STRIKE: TROOPS GUARDING MEAT TRAINS

Following the panic of 1893 came reduction in wages, and in the Pullman company's works near Chicago a great strike ensued. Governor Altgeld, sympathetic to labor, refused to call out the militia and eventually Cleveland sent federal troops to release the tie-up of trains. After the strike the public showed plainly that it was irked by both capital and labor for causing costly strikes, the expenses for which came out of the nation's pocket.

FROM "HARPER'S WEEKLY" FOR JULY 28, 1894.

271

COXEY'S ARMY

Numerous panaceas were proposed to relieve distress following the panic of 1893. One of these, made by Jacob S. Coxey, was to issue $500,000,000 in currency and with it pay for road construction. It would, he said, relieve unemployment, give the nation good roads, and allow distressed debtors to pay off their obligations. The "General," in a novel publicity stunt, gathered about one hundred men and started a march on Washington. On May 1, 1894, at the Capitol, the leaders were arrested for trespassing on the grass.

FROM "HARPER'S WEEKLY" FOR MAY 12, 1894.

THE WORLD'S FAIR OF 1893

While the country was in the midst of the depression of 1893 there was held at Chicago the Columbian Exposition, popularly called the World's Fair, to celebrate the 400th anniversary of the landing of Columbus. Beautifully laid out on the shore of Lake Michigan, the principal buildings were of unusual architectural beauty. The possibilities of electrical illumination had only recently been fully realized. To many, the exposition, in addition to being a remarkable industrial exhibit was, at night, fairyland realized.

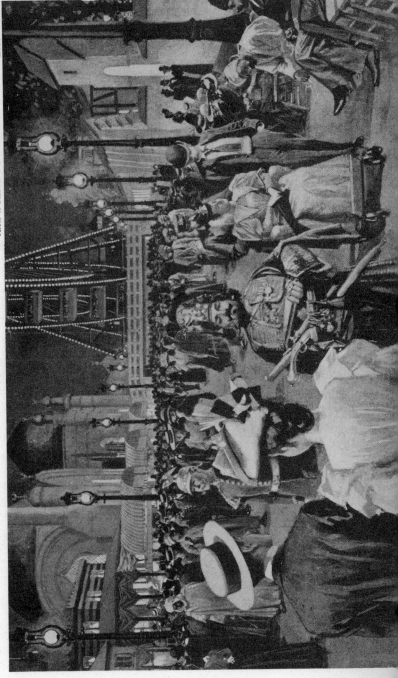

FROM A DRAWING BY THULSTRUP IN "HARPER'S WEEKLY."

RISE OF THE NAVY: THE "WHITE SQUADRON"

The Act of 1883 marks the beginning of the rise of the American Navy to first-rank power. The picture shows the so-called White Squadron of the resuscitated fleet in 1889. The presence of the masts is accounted for by the fact that the debate over sails continued almost to 1900. The renaissance was given enormous impetus by Admiral Alfred T. Mahan who, in his able and widely read books, showed for the first time the great importance of sea power as a decisive factor in history.

BRYAN AND 16 TO 1

FROM "HARPER'S WEEKLY" FOR AUGUST 22, 1896.

In 1896 bimetalism and the proposal to establish silver at a ratio of 16 to 1 to gold was the paramount issue, with the young Democrats of the South and West in open revolt against their party. All they needed was a leader. They found and acclaimed him in William Jennings Bryan who, at the Democratic Convention in a famous speech cried out, "You shall not press down upon the brow of labor this crown of thorns; you shall not crucify mankind upon a cross of gold." He won the nomination.

275

FROM "HARPER'S WEEKLY" FOR AUGUST 29, 1896.

McKINLEY AND GOLD: A FRONT-PORCH SPEECH

The millionaire politician from Cleveland, Marcus A. Hanna, was responsible for securing the Republican nomination for William McKinley on a gold standard platform. It was a violent campaign with Bryan going to the people in a nationwide tour, a method of vote-getting which was to become the accepted thing in subsequent Presidential contests. Bryan was defeated but not subdued. He was to remain the leader of the Democratic party for many years. The picture shows McKinley receiving a delegation on his front porch, a method of campaigning in sharp contrast to that of Bryan.

276

THE KLONDIKE GOLD RUSH OF 1896

In the midst of the gold-silver campaign sensational deposits of the yellow metal were discovered in the Klondike region of western Canada in August, 1896. Then started the most picturesque gold rush in all history. This unusual photograph of the actual rush shows hundreds of gold seekers camped in the snow while others push on over rugged Chilkoot Pass. Thirty thousand from all parts of the country joined in the frantic search for the yellow metal.

277

FROM "HARPER'S WEEKLY" FOR AUGUST 13, 1898.

HAWAII ANNEXED: THE PROCLAMATION READ IN HONOLULU

In 1882 the reigning king of Hawaii proclaimed a constitution granting suffrage to whites as well as to natives. Its repeal in 1893 by Queen Liliuo-kalani was followed by a revolution. The queen was deposed and an invitation extended to the United States for annexation. No action to that end was taken until 1898 when, following the Spanish-American War, the desirability of an American mid-Pacific naval base became apparent and Hawaii was annexed as a territory.

PILGRIMS OF THE PLAINS

The Civil War only checked the westward flow of our civilization. After the war this increased greatly, augmented by the flood of immigration from Europe. For a time this wave of settlement jumped over the vast plains between the Mississippi and the Rockies, first, because scanty rainfall made farming there none too easy, and second, because in that section the Indian was still at large, resolved to make a last stand against civilization.

MINING IN THE WEST: A STREET IN LEADVILLE

The activities of prospectors continued to be a powerful influence in opening certain parts of the West. In 1859 the famous Comstock Lode was discovered in Nevada. The wealth of this bonanza mine was enormous and for a time it produced half of the silver mined in the United States. By 1886 most of its mines were abandoned and it had given way to the Leadville district in Colorado which in one year yielded $11,000,000 worth of the white metal.

THE COUNTRY STORE

The country store filled a place in American life so long as the old farm existed. The coming of the railroad, more efficient farm machinery and, much later, the automobile, made an end of the general store as a universal American institution. Above all, the store was a meeting place. Round its pot-bellied stove, glowing-red on winter days, and its coal scuttle which served as a spittoon, gossip, news, politics, and the crops were discussed.

© CURTIS PUBLISHING COMPANY

281

THE COMMON SCHOOL

The great desire of the late 19th century farmer was to give his children the education that had been denied him in the pioneer days. Almost every district in the West saw that it had its tiny school building. To this boys and girls came, often over many miles of rough roads or no roads at all, to be given the bare fundamentals of an education. All ages, from toddlers up to eighteen and twenty, were taught in one room. In such schools many children, some of them destined to become the best-known men and women in the country, received their only schooling.

MACHINERY ON THE FARM

Machinery made it possible to put great areas of the West under successful cultivation. Almost every decade from the time of the first McCormick reaper witnessed improvements in the art of husbandry. Not the least of these was the development of the harvesting and threshing combine in the 1880's. The picture shows farm hands and machinery ready to move on in the wheat section of the northwest. The traveling harvest hand was a type of labor unknown before the Civil War.

FROM "HARPER'S WEEKLY" FOR DECEMBER 13, 1890.

FROM "HARPER'S WEEKLY" FOR OCTOBER 17, 1868.

THE COUNTRY CHURCH

The years after the Civil War were those in which the churches of America came to maturity. While the older and stronger organizations were increasing their memberships, a great many smaller sects also came into prominence. The most influential factor in the religious life of the rural community remained the country church where, in horse and buggy, came the townspeople and the country folk dressed in their Sunday best to worship and meet their friends and neighbors.

284

THE COUNTY FAIR

Unlike the first fairs held in this country, which were for the sale and exchange of goods, county fairs were held to exhibit the finest products of the farm. Prizes were offered for everything from pies to bulls and the competition was keen. Horse races, side shows, barkers, and all the rest, were added to make the fair more exciting. Eventually the idea was enlarged to embrace the state and these widened the farmer's contacts with the outside world.

FROM A DRAWING MADE ON STONE IN 1886 BY LOUIS MAURER.

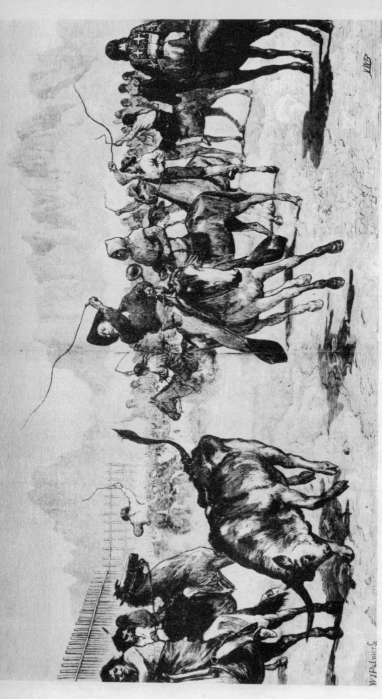

THE COW COUNTRY AND THE COWBOY

The first settlers after the pioneers ignored the so-called "American desert," but once the possibilities of ranching had been proved the great cow country sprang into existence from Texas northward and from the Missouri River to the Rockies. Its most colorful character was the cowboy, the last of the American frontier types. With all his faults the cowboy developed a code that demanded honest and courageous living in order to survive, beset as he was by Indians, horse thieves, and unscrupulous adventurers.

SINKING OF THE "MAINE"

Spanish rule in Cuba, rightly or wrongly, stirred in Americans the desire to see that country free. A financial interest in the island, which was no larger than Spain's, also influenced our attitude. The sinking of the battleship *Maine* in Havana harbor on February 15, 1898, with a loss of two hundred and sixty men, raised a storm that could not be resisted, despite McKinley's efforts to keep peace. The people of the United States wanted war, and an end of Spanish rule in the western world.

BATTLE OF MANILA BAY

The military part of the war divides into two sections. The first of these was against Spain's possessions in the Pacific. Admiral George Dewey met part of the enemy's fleet at Manila Bay in the Philippine Islands on May 1, 1898, and completely destroyed it. He could do nothing further until August 13, when, a land force having been sent him, he occupied the city of Manila. Thus did we come to have a hand in the international problems of the Pacific.

TROOPS LANDING IN CUBA

The second half of the war was in Cuba. The finest vessels in the Spanish fleet under Admiral Cervera had gone to Santiago, whence he intended to sail and then menace the Atlantic ports. Before he could escape, however, he was bottled up by the American navy under Commodore Winfield S. Schley and later under Admiral William T. Sampson. The best known incident of the blockade was the exploit of Lieutenant Richard P. Hobson and six men in sinking the *Merrimac* in the harbor's channel. They volunteered, thinking death almost a certainty, but they escaped and became national heroes. Again nothing could be done before there was a land force, and Sampson requested troops. On June 22d they began to come ashore under General William R. Shafter. They included the famous Rough Riders (without horses) under Leonard Wood, with Theodore Roosevelt second-in-command.

TROOPS ENTRENCHED AT SAN JUAN HILL

On July first came the attack on the city of Santiago. The first advance on the outlying village of El Caney was delayed by a brave but greatly outnumbered Spanish force. Finally it was successful. Meanwhile the second half of the attack on San Juan Hill had likewise been delayed by stubborn opposition. Eventually, without orders, the Americans charged and annihilated the tiny band of defenders. The city itself did not surrender until July 17th when, Cervera's fleet having been destroyed, its doom became inevitable.

291

BATTLE OF SANTIAGO

On July 3rd, Cervera, not willing to surrender his fleet without a battle, decided to run for it. Bravely he led the procession out of Santiago harbor. Once in the open, instead of scattering, the Spanish ships gave battle, but either their powder was poor or their aim was bad, and it soon became clear that the struggle was an unequal one. Within four hours Cervera lost every one of his ships. Throughout the war the navy showed to better advantage than the land forces, due to the fact that the latter were poorly equipped.

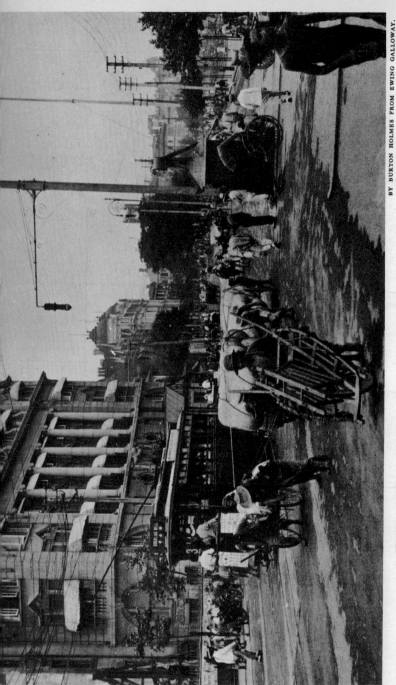

THE "OPEN DOOR" POLICY: THE OLD SHANGHAI BUND

BY BURTON HOLMES FROM EWING GALLOWAY.

John Hay, Secretary of State under McKinley, won what was apparently a great diplomatic victory at a time when the European Powers were establishing themselves in vast zones "leased" from the helpless government of China and threatening exclusion of American trade. In September, 1899, Secretary Hay secured the consent of the powers to refrain from interference with Chinese customs collections at any of the twenty-two treaty ports, and to open their "spheres of influence," to other nations. Unfortunately, the beneficial effects anticipated for the "open door" policy proved to be in some degree illusory.

THE BOXER OUTBREAK: THE AMERICAN REFUGE

Early in 1900, foreign residents in China found themselves in the midst of a rebellion sponsored by a secret society known as "The Boxers," with the purpose of expelling all outsiders from Chinese soil. Missionaries were murdered, while at Pekin the inmates of the legations defended themselves for weeks in enclosures such as that shown above. Troops of several nations landed, defeated the Chinese, and rescued the besieged legations. The powers imposed territorial and financial indemnities on China, the United States eventually returning its share. American moderation in the matter did much to promote friendly relations with the Chinese.

© C. A. KILLIE.

NORTHERN PACIFIC PANIC

An effort of the Harriman interests to secure control of Northern Pacific securities resulted in a clash with the Hill-Morgan financial group. The financial battle culminated in the panic of May 9, 1901, when Northern Pacific common soared to $1000 on the Stock Exchange. Harriman secured a majority interest in the road, but control of the common was retained by Hill and the matter was settled by formation of the Northern Securities Company, later dissolved by the Supreme Court.

FROM THE "NEW YORK HERALD," MAY 9, 1901.

GIANTS OF WALL STREET, IN FIERCE BATTLE FOR MASTERY, PRECIPITATE CRASH THAT BRINGS RUIN TO HORDE OF PYGMI

HENRY M. FLAGLER
IN ACTIONS FOR DOLLARS AND DIVORCE
SUED BY A HUSBAND

Edward C. Foote, an Express Agent, Demands $100,000 from Standard Oil Man, Charging Him with Having Alienated His Wife's Affections.

SAID TO HAVE GIVEN HER RICH PRESENTS

Divorce Proceedings Also Begun, Naming Two Other Corespondents, One Being Husband Whom the Woman Married After Obtaining a Divorce in South Dakota.

WHEN NORTHERN PACIFIC REACHED 1000.

PANIC AND DISTRESS MARK THE ENDING GREAT STOCK B

Kuhn-Loeb-Harriman Syndicate's with Hill-Morgan Interests, sult in Unnumbered "Shorts Being Driven Sharply to the Wall.

TITANIC STRUGGLE GED OVER NORTHERN PA

Common Stock Fluctuated Betwee and 145, Jumping Five Points Way with Lightninglike Rapi ity, and Closing at 160.

ONLY "STRONG" STOCK ON LIST NET GAIN WAS 16 1-2 F

294

BEGINNING OF THE MOVIES

The above scene is from the first motion picture to embody a plot, "The Great Train Robbery," an adaptation of fiction to the screen by one of Thomas A. Edison's staff. It was a momentous day for America when, in 1903, this primitive forerunner of today's "epics" was shown. It was the injection of a story which started the public flocking to early theaters, known as "nickelodeons" because of the price of admission. The story-picture created a great new industry and exerted a deep influence on civilization, with the future still undefined.

FORMATION OF THE I. W. W.

Regarding Socialist doctrines as too peaceful, a group of advocates of "direct action" organized the Industrial Workers of the World in Chicago in 1905. For years the extreme "left-wingers" had been active in an unorganized way, and had engaged in riots such as the one shown below in Tompkins Square, New York, in the middle seventies. The new organization was promptly repudiated by the Socialists and the labor unions. The World War brought about the decline of the movement.

FROM "FRANK LESLIE'S ILLUSTRATED NEWSPAPER" FOR JANUARY 31. 1874.

THE RISE OF LABOR:
SAMUEL GOMPERS

Organized labor's growth to national
influence occurred during the early
nineteen-hundreds under the adroit
leadership of Samuel Gompers, a
former London cigar-maker's appren-
tice. Early reforms included the eight-
hour law for Government workers,
the ten-hour law for street railway
employees. The designation of the first
Monday in September as "Labor
Day," a national holiday, was another
of Gompers' achievements. Such were
his abilities, that during the years of
his presidency, 1882–1924 (with the
exception of one year), the American
Federation of Labor became a potent
factor in the economic, industrial, and
political life of the country.

RAILROAD REGULATION: THE HEPBURN ACT

Passage of the Hepburn Act, June 29, 1906, by Congress imposed severe penalties on railroad rebating and unjust discrimination against shippers. The Interstate Commerce Commission was empowered to prescribe rates, subject to court review, and schedules of all tariffs were required to be filed with that body, which was also authorized to prescribe a uniform method of keeping accounts of the common carriers. Issuance of free passes was restricted to families of employees of the transportation companies. Express companies, sleeping-car companies, and oil pipe lines were also brought under the I. C. C. The picture shows the great freight yards of the Illinois Central in Chicago.

FOOD AND DRUG REGULATION AND INSPECTION

By the dawn of the Twentieth Century, adulteration of food articles, medicines and packing products had become so widespread as to constitute a national abuse. In 1906, Congress enacted legislation to cover interstate commerce in such commodities, prohibiting the manufacture and sale of those containing harmful substances, and compelling truthful labeling. On the same day that the Pure Food and Drugs Act was passed, Congress also placed the slaughtering and preparation of meats to be shipped over state lines subject to inspection by the Department of Agriculture. The picture shows part of the great stockyards of the meat packers, Armour & Co., in Chicago.

THE PANAMA CANAL

Defeated by yellow fever and malaria, a French company had abandoned construction of an inter-ocean canal across the Isthmus of Panama in 1889. With establishment of the Republic of Panama, the United States took up the work where the French left off. Sanitary measures inaugurated by Dr. William C. Gorgas ended the fever menace and saved thousands of workers' lives. The entire nation watched with pride the progress of the Army construction work. On August 15, 1914, the canal was opened to traffic of all nations. The photograph shows work on the Culebra Cut in 1908.

300

BY HINE FROM EWING GALLOWAY.

IMMIGRATION REACHES ITS CREST

Immigration to the United States touched a high mark by June, 1907, with admission of almost 1,300,000 aliens for the fiscal year. A movement which had been in progress for many decades had culminated, bringing in its wake important social changes and serious domestic problems. Although the tide that had engulfed the country was to recede, it was not to be finally checked until after the war. Above is a pre-war scene at Ellis Island, debarkation point for immigrants in New York.

KNICKERBOCKER TRUST CO.
AND BROKERS SUSPEND;
$68,000,000 INVOLVED.

Day of Apprehension in the Financial District Marked by the Closing of the Barney Concern, the Failure of Mayer & Co., a Big Brokerage House, and a Smash in Prices on the Stock Exchange.

FAILURE TO EXTEND PROMISED AID FORCES KNICKERBOCKER TO QUIT.

Much Doubt Felt Whether the Big Trust Company Will Resume—$8,000,000 Withdrawn in Run by Excited Depositors—State Officials May Take Charge of the Concern—Secretary Cortelyou Here to Consider the Situation—May Extend Government Aid—Clearing House Banks Declared Sound.

During a day bordering on widespread financial New York yesterday witnessed the suspension of the Knickerbocker Trust Company, with deposits aggregating more than $62,000,000, and the failure of the ...

FLYING DOUGHNUTS STOP CHURCH SALE.

Pastor Campbell Dodges 'Em, but Sexton Is Hit—Woman Does the Throwing.

FROM THE "NEW YORK AMERICAN" FOR OCTOBER 23, 1907.

THE PANIC OF 1907

A ten-year period of overcapitalization ended in the panic of October 22, 1907, when gilt-edged securities took an abrupt downward plunge following the closing of the Knickerbocker Trust Co. Wall Street interests charged that the Roosevelt policy of strict enforcement of regulations governing corporations was the cause, and the President countered that infractions of the law by corporations, not enforcement, were responsible. It advertised, however, the failure of the Currency Act of 1900 to stabilize the currency. It was short-lived and never became widespread.

302

THE FLEET SAILS ROUND THE WORLD

Resentment at increased Japanese immigration to the Pacific coast reached a high-water mark, especially among the newspapers and the labor elements in the West, in 1908. Perhaps as a warning, and to give the world a demonstration of American naval strength, President Roosevelt sent a fleet of twenty-eight war- ships in December for a round-the-world voyage, which was completed in February, 1909, without accident. At every port of call, including Yokohama, the personnel were received with enthusiasm and a cordial welcome, the President terming them "heralds of peace." The picture shows the fleet at San Francisco.

ADVENT OF THE AUTOMOBILE

To derisive cries of "Get a Horse" and a popular song, "Get Out and Get Under," the horseless carriage began to appear more frequently on the nation's crude highways as 1908 approached. After the first wave of popular resentment, the future possibilities of this new means of travel were quickly recognized and a new industry sprang into being. The transformation worked on the social habits of the country is still going on. The little boy perched on the back of this early automobile is Clarence Chamberlin, later to be famous as a transatlantic flyer.

AMERICAN CONTROL WITHDRAWN FROM CUBA

The provision of an orderly government in Cuba was one of the major problems resulting from the Spanish-American War. Europe frankly doubted our pledge to turn the island over to its people once they were able to conduct their affairs as a nation. From 1899 to 1902, General Leonard Wood carried out the work of establishing the new government, including a system of public education. Major Walter Reed stamped out yellow fever with his experiments proving that the mosquito transmitted the disease. The first Cuban general election was held in February, 1902, and on May 20th General Wood turned over the government to President Tomas Estrada Palma. The United States intervened in Cuba in 1906 and also in 1912 and 1917 to restore order or prevent revolutions threatening foreign interests, and has occasionally landed Marines. For years our policy in the island was dictated by the so-called Platt Amendment of 1901 which gave us the right to intervene to preserve independence, order, republican government, and to see that Cuba discharged her obligations to other nations. One of the policies sponsored by Franklin Roosevelt was the repeal of the Platt Amendment. The picture shows the United States fleet in Havana harbor after the Spanish-American War.

THE BRYAN–CHAMORRO TREATY WITH NICARAGUA

Toward the close of Taft's administration Nicaragua offered to sell the United States the exclusive right to build a canal through that country and to establish forts at each end in return for $3,000,000. When William Jennings Bryan became Secretary of State, he sought to amend the offer so as to make Nicaragua an American protectorate. The Senate at Washington refused to approve this, and the Bryan-Chamorro Treaty of 1916 was confined to the original terms of 1912. The picture shows Nicaraguan rebels fighting loyal troops near Nicaragua.

THE CAMPAIGN OF 1912: ROOSEVELT NOMINATED AT THE
BULL MOOSE CONVENTION

The national campaign of 1912, marked by bitter personalities, saw Theodore Roosevelt again a candidate, splitting the Republican ranks with his Progressive, or Bull Moose, party. Taft, candidate for re-election, ran a poor third in the voting, which placed Woodrow Wilson, scholarly Democratic reformer, in the White House. It was the first Democratic victory since Cleveland's election, and was aided by many erstwhile Republicans.

THE INCOME TAX AMENDMENT

The Underwood Tariff of 1913 embodied a tax on all incomes as a means of compensating for decreases in customs revenues provided by the act. The income tax idea was not new, having been used during the Civil War, although an attempt to impose one in 1895 was declared unconstitutional by a 5 to 4 Supreme Court decision. This led ultimately to the Sixteenth Amendment to the Constitution. With some lapses, the general trend of income-tax rates has been upward, some states even imposing levies of their own.

POPULAR ELECTION OF SENATORS

The framers of the Constitution provided that Senators should be elected by state legislatures. Attempts to change this were immediate, but always met with defeat despite House victories. In 1904 Oregon permitted voters to indicate their Senatorial choice on ballots, and the movement spread until enough states to ratify a constitutional amendment were following this example. The Senate yielded in 1911, and the amendment calling for direct popular election of its members was ratified by three-fourths of the states and proclaimed part of the Constitution on May 31, 1913. The picture shows Bryan signing the announcement of the Seventeenth Amendment.

THE FEDERAL RESERVE ACT

Growth of the currency and banking problem brought about the Federal Reserve Act of December 23, 1913, by which the country was divided into twelve districts with a member bank in a central city in each. All national banks were required to enter the reserve system, which provided for acceptance of approved "paper" in exchange for Federal Reserve notes whenever expansion of the currency is required by business conditions. Although advocates of the Act encountered widespread resistance, it has since proved its worth in coping with the ever-fluctuating business and financial conditions of the country. The picture shows, right, the Federal Reserve bank in New York.

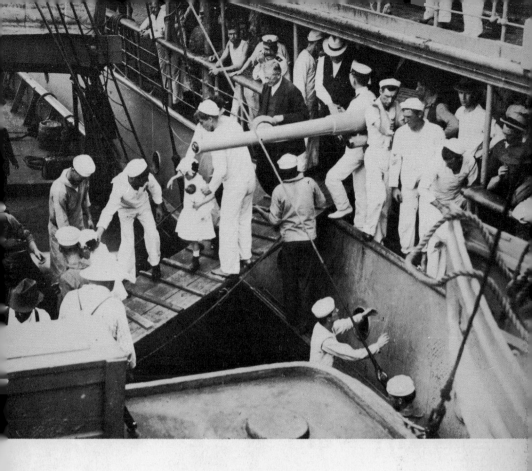

THE OCCUPATION OF VERA CRUZ

In 1913, Victoriano Huerta was president of Mexico, his henchmen having murdered his predecessor. To combat the usurper, President Wilson raised the embargo on arms to revolutionists fighting the Huerta regime. In April, 1914, sailors from the U. S. S. *Dolphin*, landing at Tampico to buy gasoline, were arrested and detained by Huerta's officers, and the United States, obtaining their release, demanded a salute to our flag as formal apology. Huerta refused, and the battleships *Utah* and *Florida* shelled the arsenal at Vera Cruz and landed Marines who captured the city. Huerta eventually resigned and left Mexico. Above, transferring refugees from Vera Cruz to our warships.

THE PANAMA-PACIFIC INTERNATIONAL EXPOSITION

This exposition, held in San Francisco in 1915, celebrated the opening of the Panama Canal and the quatercentenary of the discovery of the Pacific. On February 6th, President Wilson pushed a gold button in Washington, which set the mechanical exhibits in motion. The location extended for about two and a half miles along San Francisco Bay. Eleven splendid buildings housed the exhibits.

THE OCCUPATION OF HAITI

American control of the finances of Santo Domingo, under the Roosevelt arrangement of 1905, was challenged by President Jiménez in 1916, and the naval forces took over the Dominican government. When the republic of Haiti refused to permit establishment of a similar financial protectorate, Marines were landed in December, 1914. Under our military occupancy the Haitian government was stabilized and a new constitution drafted. The occupation met with resistance which was finally stamped out by the Marines and the newly organized Haitian gendarmerie. The picture shows a street in Port-au-Prince.

313

THE FUTILE CHASE OF VILLA

Huerta's successor as Mexican President, Carranza, was opposed by the bandit chief, Pancho Villa who, during Wilson's period of "Watchful Waiting" on the Mexican situation, met our troops on the border under friendly circumstances, and below is shown with Brigadier General Pershing. But on March 10, 1916, a horde of Villistas raided Columbus, New Mexico, killing soldiers and citizens. Pershing was sent with a punitive expedition to catch the bandits, but the wily Villa eluded pursuit in the mountain fastnesses south of the border. The expedition was withdrawn, and Carranza gained temporary control of Mexico's turbulent politics.

314

PURCHASE OF THE VIRGIN ISLANDS

The process of building up a protective system of naval stations and strategic points to guard the Panama Canal from the east was augmented on January 17, 1917, when the United States purchased the Virgin Island group, guarding the northeastern entrance of the Caribbean. The kingdom of Denmark, which had owned them, was paid $25,000,000, and the inhabitants of the islands, of whom 90 percent are Negroes, were placed under the government of an American naval officer. Above is a street scene in St. Thomas.

THE GALVESTON FLOOD: WRECKAGE

A West Indian hurricane, blowing at the rate of 135 miles an hour, struck the prosperous city of Galveston, Texas, on September 8, 1900, and caused a loss of life estimated at 6,000, and property damage of $15,000,000. Waters of the Gulf of Mexico, whipped to fury by the wind, flooded the streets to a depth higher than a man's head. The nation poured assistance to the stricken survivors and distribution of relief was supervised by troops, hastily sent to the scene of disaster.

ASSASSINATION OF McKINLEY

While shaking hands with visitors to the Pan-American Exposition at Buffalo, on September 6, 1901, President McKinley was shot twice and fatally wounded by Leon Czolgosz, a Russian-Polish anarchist; who had carried a pistol under a handkerchief wrapped around his hand. The President died September 14th, Vice-President Theodore Roosevelt thereupon taking the oath as President. Czolgosz was duly tried, found guilty of murder and executed. The photograph, one of McKinley's last, shows him at the Exposition the day before he was shot.

MAN CONQUERS THE AIR

Practical aviation started December 17, 1903, when, in the presence of five spectators, the Wright brothers, Orville and Wilbur, made the first flights in a controllable heavier-than-air machine at Kitty Hawk, North Carolina. At the same time the Wrights were experimenting, Samuel P. Langley was also working on his aërodrome but his machine did not leave the ground till years afterward, and then possibly with some mechanisms not developed by him at the time.

BURNING OF THE "GENERAL SLOCUM"

A terrible disaster which shocked the entire country was the burning of the excursion steamer *General Slocum* on June 15, 1904, in the Hell Gate passage of the East River at New York City. Out of about 1800 passengers, over 1000, mostly women and children out to enjoy a picnic and a day on the water, lost their lives. The boat was old and unseaworthy, and lifeboats and life preservers in wretched condition. The captain was later convicted of criminal negligence. The photograph shows the vessel as she lay on the river's bottom, her superstructure still smouldering.

319

SAN FRANCISCO EARTHQUAKE AND FIRE

On April 18, 1906, an earthquake never before equaled in violence in the United States struck the city of San Francisco. Soon afterward fires broke out all over the city and for the next three days it was a raging inferno. Troops dynamited large areas in an effort to stop the flames. Said a New York newspaper: "She is the most bunged-up town that ever was. But the spirit of her is enough to bring tears to an American's eyes." Within a year the stricken section was being rebuilt in a new and more beautiful form.

NORTH POLE DISCOVERED

The flag of the United States was planted on top of the world on April 6, 1909, by Commander Robert E. Peary, after years of futile efforts by other explorers to attain the Pole. Worldwide acclaim greeted the exploit, although Dr. Frederick Cook, a Brooklyn scientist, disputed Peary's priority. Ultimately Perry's claim was upheld, Cook's discredited. The photograph shows Peary on the *Roosevelt*, the ship that carried him to the North.

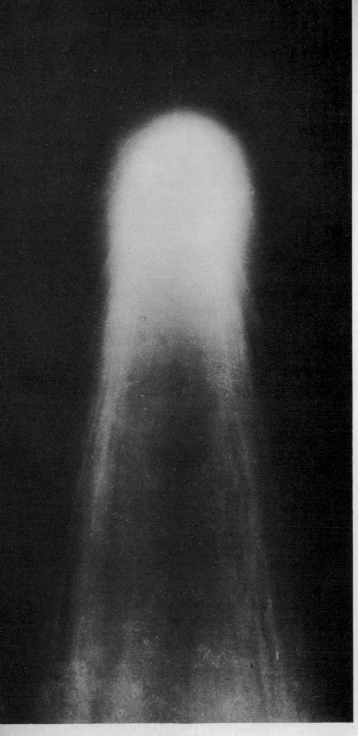

HALLEY'S COMET: JOHN DOE STUDIES ASTRONOMY

During April, 1910, the periodic 75 year visibility of Halley's Comet, a heavenly body of extraordinary brilliance, was ·attended by widespread publicity and consequent popular interest of an unprecedented sort. The comet became the theme of articles, conversation, and even comedy, as well as of unusual scientific activity. Due to technical progress, a wealth of data on the infrequent visitor was obtained by the great observatories, and the man in the street given a glimpse of worlds beyond his own.

SINKING OF THE "TITANIC"

Westward bound on her maiden voyage, the great liner *Titanic*, largest of its day, struck an iceberg in the North Atlantic on April 14, 1912, and sank with a loss of about 1000 persons. America and Europe were plunged into mourning, but thrilled by reports of heroism aboard the sinking ship. Wireless telegraphy was credited with the summoning of aid where in the past the number of those saved might have been negligible. The photographs show survivors being picked up by the *Carpathia*.

THE INCIDENT AT SARAJEVO

The assassination, on June 28, 1914, of the Archduke Franz Ferdinand, heir
to the Austrian throne, and his wife while visiting Sarajevo in Bosnia,
proved to be the match that started the European conflagration. Holding
Serbian revolutionists responsible for the murder, Austria declared war.
Russia mobilized, and Germany thereupon declared war on Russia. France,
Russia's ally, became embroiled. The German invasion of Belgium brought
Great Britain into the conflict. Soon most of Europe was under arms. The
illustration shows the Archduke and Duchess a few minutes before they
were slain.

SINKING OF THE "LUSITANIA"

When 114 American men, women, and children perished in the torpedoing of the giant Cunarder *Lusitania* off the Old Head of Kinsale, Ireland, on May 7, 1915, the entire nation was aroused. Altogether 1153 aboard the liner perished when she fell prey to a German U-Boat. On the morning she sailed, the above notice appeared in American newspapers. President Wilson sent a note on May 13th, asking the German Government to disavow the sinking. The German reply deprecated the loss of American lives, but denied responsibility. The picture was the last one of the vessel, taken when she was stopped by a British merchant cruiser and given instructions as to how best to evade the submarines.

THE FORD PEACE EXPEDITION

One of the most amazing, in retrospect, efforts to end the war was under-taken by Henry Ford in 1915. Although not an active pacifist he was con-vinced by others that he could put an end to the great European conflict if the right gesture were made. He chartered the ship *Oscar II* and sailed to Christiania, Norway, whence, finally convinced that the war must run its course, he returned home.

PREPAREDNESS, AND A FAMOUS CASE

Some far-sighted persons realized before 1917 that we should prepare for war. Meetings and parades were held to further this cause, during one of which in San Francisco on July 22, 1916, a bomb exploded killing six people. Thomas Mooney, a labor leader, was sentenced to death for the crime. The sentence was never carried out and Mooney is still in jail claiming, among other things, that he watched the parade from the roof shown in this picture.

WARRING ON A NEUTRAL

Due to the tight British blockade, Germany and Austria were unable to obtain supplies from the United States, while the Allies secured them easily. A series of mysterious outrages, such as the Black Tom explosion below, finding of bombs on munition ships consigned to Allied ports, and blowing up of bridges on the Canadian border, led to a Secret Service investigation. A letter from Dr. Dumba, Austrian ambassador at Washington, was intercepted, revealing plots to disorganize the supplying of the Allies. On demand of the State Department, Dumba was recalled, and with him the German attachés, Captains Von Papen and Boy-Ed.

328

WILSON'S REËLECTION AND UNRESTRICTED SUBMARINE WARFARE

Reëlected on the slogan of "He kept us out of war," President Wilson was confronted on January 31, 1917, with Germany's declaration of unrestricted submarine warfare against all ships, regardless of nationality, entering the war zone. This breach of a previous pledge not to destroy merchant ships without warning or saving of human lives the President met by breaking off diplomatic relations with Germany. The President then ordered the arming of our merchant ships. The picture shows the President in his second inaugural parade.

329

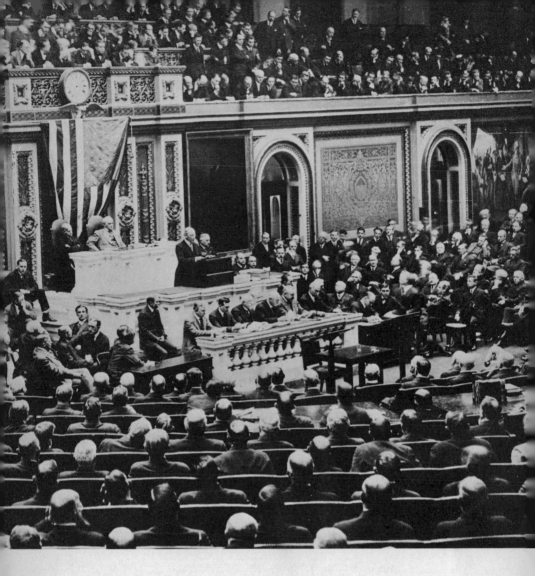

READING THE WAR MESSAGE

Night in the House Chamber at the Capitol, April 2, 1917. In ringing
tones the President declared that the "irresponsible German government
has cast aside all considerations of humanity" and that its recent actions
had been "nothing less than war against the government and people of the
United States." "The world must be made safe for democracy . . ." The
Senate by a vote of 86 to 6, the House by 373 to 50 (after a sixteen-hour
debate) passed the resolution declaring war on Germany early in the morning of Good Friday, April 6, 1917.

THE SELECTIVE DRAFT

On recommendation of the General Staff, Congress on May 18, 1917, passed the Selective Service Act, requiring all males between the ages of 21 and 31 to register for selective military service. Of the first numbers drafted, about half were retained and sent to sixteen huge base camps in as many states. The National Guard, mustered into Federal service, occupied sixteen others. Parades of the men chosen in the draft were held in many cities before their departure for the training camps.

UNITED STATES SIGNAL CORPS PHOTO.

TRAINING CAMPS

The speed with which raw citizens were given the fundamental war training was amazing. The army command
emphasized, among other things, three principles in the
training of American soldiers: they should be drilled to
fight without interlarding with foreign troops, they should be expert in the use of the bayonet, and the
artillery should be expert in marksmanship. In a word,
the recruits were trained for offensive, independent
fighting.

SAYING GOOD-BY

There had been nothing since the Civil War to compare with the wave of patriotic frenzy that swept the country as the troops were bade farewell for the last time. Despite recent attempts to discredit both our motives for entering the conflict and the agencies which stirred these motives, it remains true that we could only have avoided war by ignoring offensive acts against us the like of which few neutrals had ever before been subjected to. Popular enthusiasms at the time, including those of the women, were for the war.

333

BUILDING A MERCHANT MARINE: HOG ISLAND

From January to July, 1917, the U-boats took fearful toll of the world's shipping. To counteract this loss, the United States Shipping Board organized the Emergency Fleet Corporation and every shipyard in the country was put at top speed. By standardizing designs, inland steel plants turned out parts for these ships, assembly going on at seaboard points such as Hog Island, shown above, with six ships often being launched in a day.

334

THE LIBERTY LOANS

The cost of the war put an unprecedented burden of taxation on the nation, and to meet this, unprecedented taxes were necessary, culminating in the House Revenue Bill of the autumn of 1918 calling for six billion dollars. In May, 1917, the Government offered two billion dollars' worth of its bonds to the general public at $3\frac{1}{2}$ per cent, in the First Liberty Loan. Like the four others that followed, it was oversubscribed. The bonds were sold in units of as little as $50, and there were few people who did not invest their savings in them. The President is shown parading in the cause of the 4th Loan.

THE TRANSATLANTIC FERRY

Protected by the convoy system perfected by the Navy, thousands of
American troops were safely transported to France and back again in one
of the war's greatest mass movements. Among the huge liners were many
ex-German ships, seized after long internment Although their crews had
wrecked their engines, American workmen reconditioned them successfully
Towering among them was the *Vaterland*, shown here, largest ship of its
day, re-named the *Leviathan*.

"LAFAYETTE, WE ARE HERE!"

The military power of the West set foot on French soil in the person of the commander-in-chief of the American Expeditionary Force, General John J. Pershing, when he stepped ashore at Boulogne, in 1917. Shortly afterward he won his first battle when he successfully opposed the proposal of the Allied staff to apportion American troops to various combatant armies, thus preserving the integrity of the American Army as a fighting unit.

THE AMERICANS COME

Of the 2,000,000 United States troops who made the voyage to the war zone in long columns of transports only a few hundreds were lost at sea. This was the great part played by the Navy in the war. The most serious single incident was the loss of the Cunard steamship *Tuscania*, torpedoed off the coast of Ireland in February, 1918, when 175 Americans were drowned. The rest of the men aboard the vessel were rescued by the convoying vessels.

THE LAFAYETTE ESCADRILLE

Many young Americans whose sympathies were with the French before America entered the war, offered their services as aviators in the French Army, forming a unit known as the Lafayette Escadrille, which earned a name for courageous and resourceful fighting against the German airmen. Norman Prince was most active in its organization, and Raoul Lufbery became one of its most famous flyers. With America's entry into the conflict, many transferred to the American air service. In January, 1918, the organization became a part of the American Army.

THE YANKS' FIRST BLOW: CANTIGNY

The doughboy had his first taste of battle at Cantigny. To the First Division went the credit for capture of this heavily fortified position. The military importance of the victory was not great but its moral effect was. It showed that the American soldier had been soundly trained, that he was reliable under fire, and it foreshadowed his work in the Argonne.

340

CHÂTEAU THIERRY AND BELLEAU WOOD

The last of May and early June, 1918, was one of the most critical periods of the war. The Germans were making their final attempt to break the Allied lines and open a way to Paris. In this engagement the Americans played an important part. First, on May 31st and June 1st, they prevented the Germans from crossing the Marne at Château Thierry; then they checked the advance on the Paris road itself, and ended by taking the strongly defended position in Belleau Wood. The latter was a machine gun and bayonet fight, a type of work in which Americans proved, throughout the war, to excel.

SOISSONS TURNS THE TIDE

By the middle of July, the French and Americans, the German drive checked, were ready for the ordeal of a counter-offensive. Orders to attack were secretly given. The troops were tense. Now would come the real test of Americans to conduct successfully a crushing offensive. On July 18th it began on the flank between Soissons and Château Thierry. In the five days of terrific fighting that followed the Americans and French suffered great loss, but the Germans were swept out of their trenches and in retreat. Those days were the turning point of the war. The photograph shows German dead in a sunken road far in the rear from which the enemy was driven on the second day.

WIPING OUT THE ST. MIHIEL SALIENT

Since 1914, the Germans had managed to hold a vast triangle of French territory jutting twenty miles from the Lorraine border with its apex at St. Mihiel, on the Meuse. Since July, Foch had been on the offensive. He determined to keep on it till the war was over. Sensing that he would strike at St. Mihiel, Von Hindenburg gave orders to evacuate the salient, but his commanders were slow and on September 12th Pershing struck. The photograph shows troops going toward the front.

RESULTS AT ST. MIHIEL

The artillery began pounding the enemy lines at 1 A.M. At 5 A.M. the rolling barrage began, with the Americans going "over the top," to follow it. The enemy barbed wire was cut and the front trenches reached. Said General Pershing: "At the cost of only 7000 casualties, mostly light, we had taken 16,000 prisoners . . . and established our lines in a position to threaten Metz. The Allies found (in this first offensive of the American First Army) that they had a formidable army to aid them, and the enemy learned finally that he had one to reckon with." The photograph shows German troops retreating.

344

THE MEUSE–ARGONNE: FIRST PHASE

The supreme effort of the Americans was the Meuse–Argonne offensive between late September and the Armistice. On its success hinged Foch's plans, now that he had straightened out his lines and was ready to deliver the final blow. In the last days of September and early October, green American troops went forward ten miles, penetrating the German second line of defense, although with terrific loss. It was the first phase of the battle.

THE MEUSE-ARGONNE: SECOND PHASE

The second phase included the struggle for the Argonne forest and saw the most terrific fighting that an American army had been called on to face in all its history. The Germans were resolved that wherever else they gave way, this great sector of the line, which had been theirs since 1914, would be held. Dying for every foot of ground conquered, the Americans went forward, plunging into the Argonne forest. It was there that the Lost Battalion advanced too far and was cut off from retreat. The attack reached its high point with the capture of Blanc Mont, in which the fury of the Americans was outstanding.

THE MEUSE-ARGONNE: THIRD PHASE

By November 1st, Pershing had decided to capture the remaining positions before him, not by frontal attack but by maneuver. Aided by artillery bombardment his troops went forward. By November 11th the French and Americans had joined hands. Sedan and the main German line of communication were within artillery range, and the combined Allied troops would soon be in the rear of the German armies. The greatest debacle of the war could now only be saved by an armistice.

THE ARMISTICE

The German high command now was forced to admit what they had long secretly known. The end was at hand. Armistice was declared on the 11th, amid scenes in the trenches that ranged from blank wonder and dazed inability to realize that bloodshed was at last over to scenes of wild celebration. To every soldier the ending of the war meant a turning-point in his life. Said Pershing of the Meuse-Argonne battle: "... You battered against the pivot of the enemy line ... a position fortified by four years of labor designed to render it impregnable. ... The achievement of the First Army ... is scarcely to be equaled in American history. ..."

THE NAVY'S PART

Preceded by a destroyer fleet which arrived May 4th at Queenstown, Ireland, the battleship divisions of the United States Navy were sent across the Atlantic to coöperate with the British Grand Fleet at its North Sea bases. Although our battleships fought no engagement with the German fleet, their presence aided in nullifying German sea power for the remainder of the war. Thousands of sailors aboard them witnessed the final surrender of the German warships and submarines, treacherously scuttled by their crews afterward at Scapa Flow. The picture shows Admiral Beatty and British tars welcoming the ships of the United States at Scapa Flow.

ARMISTICE DAY AT HOME

News of the signing of the Armistice brought an outpouring of the people into the streets of all American cities rejoicing at the end of the war. Men in uniform were hailed with enthusiasm, total strangers exchanged delighted handshakes. The Kaiser was "licked," Yankee-fashion, and the formidable German army had been taught to respect an aroused United States. Before homes where a gold star in the window signified one had fallen for his country, reverent groups gathered. The above picture shows Fifth Avenue in New York on November 11, 1918.

THE BIG FOUR

Knowing that his proposed Covenant of the League of Nations, one of his Fourteen Points, was being discountenanced by a hostile Congress behind him, President Wilson sailed for the Peace Conference on December 4, 1918, and on arrival at Paris commenced work on the Treaty with (left to right) Orlando of Italy, Lloyd George of Great Britain, and Clemenceau of France. The enthusiasm with which he was hailed throughout Europe has never been accorded any other individual American. He succeeded in having a committee appointed to draw up his Covenant as an integral part of the treaty of peace, more than a dozen nations expressing immediate approval, then returned to face the Congressional opposition.

HOOVER, AND RELIEF OF THE STARVING

The plight of helpless women and children in invaded Belgium resulted in the formation of the Belgian Relief Commission, which under the able direction of Herbert Hoover saved thousands of lives by its efficient distribution of food supplies. Later American relief was extended to post-war Germany and Russia. During the conflict, Serbia and other nations were helped by American generosity. With the entrance of this country into the war, Hoover was appointed Food Administrator to conserve national resources in foodstuffs. He inaugurated wheatless, meatless, and sugarless days, and directed the sending of $2,000,000,000 worth of food to Europe during 1918. He is shown here, accompanied by John D. Rockefeller, Jr., in one of the war-time cafeterias.

352

"SEE AMERICA THIRST"

This parody of an advertising catch-phrase became popular with the advent of national prohibition. Its regrettable effects on our national life would probably have been avoided had not war hysteria made it possible for the extreme temperance advocates to popularize their program. Transportation of intoxicants was also forbidden, and citizens were even searched for hip-flasks, as shown above. Prohibition was embodied in the Constitution as the Eighteenth Amendment. The era of the prohibition agent, the bootlegger, and the speakeasy was ushered into the national life.

THE PEACE CONFERENCE

On June 28, 1919, in the same Hall of Mirrors at Versailles where King William of Prussia humbled a prostrate France in 1871, the representatives of Germany signed the Treaty of Peace of the Great War, by which Alsace-Lorraine was restored to France, and other territories to Belgium, Denmark, and Poland. Germany agreed to surrender most of her fleet, to demolish her fortifications, abolish her air force, and reduce her army to a police force of 100,000 men. An initial payment of 20 billion marks to pay for damage in regions occupied by her troops was exacted, and she was compelled, under protest, to assume responsibility for the war. The new German Republic was stunned by the terms.

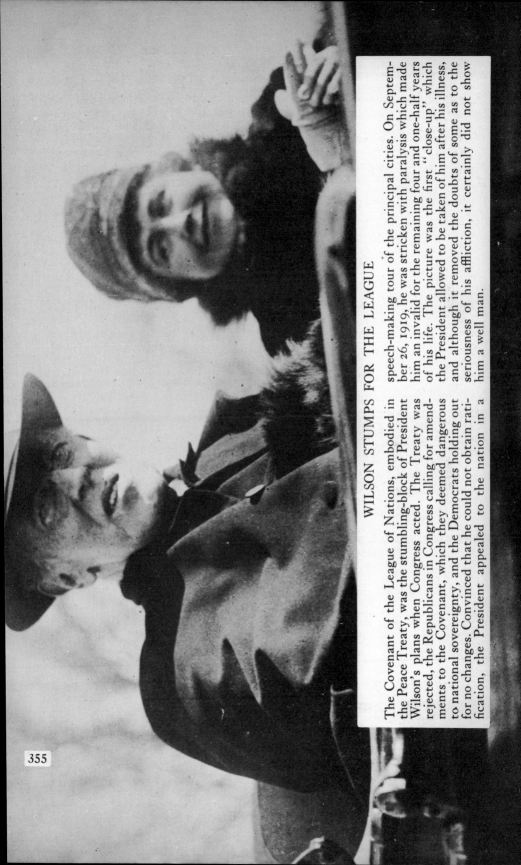

WILSON STUMPS FOR THE LEAGUE

The Covenant of the League of Nations, embodied in the Peace Treaty, was the stumbling-block of President Wilson's plans when Congress acted. The Treaty was rejected, the Republicans in Congress calling for amendments to the Covenant, which they deemed dangerous to national sovereignty, and the Democrats holding out for no changes. Convinced that he could not obtain ratification, the President appealed to the nation in a speech-making tour of the principal cities. On September 26, 1919, he was stricken with paralysis which made him an invalid for the remaining four and one-half years of his life. The picture was the first "close-up", which the President allowed to be taken of him after his illness, and although it removed the doubts of some as to the seriousness of his affliction, it certainly did not show him a well man.

THE BOSTON POLICE STRIKE

In September, 1919, the police force of Boston, after negotiating unsuccessfully for a pay increase, went on strike, thinking to bring the city to terms when it found itself without police protection. The strike was broken through the intervention of Governor Calvin Coolidge, who placed Massachusetts National Guardsmen in charge after rioting had occurred. The successful breaking of the strike, credited to Coolidge, brought him national fame, and was a potent factor in bringing about his nomination for Vice-President in 1920.

WOMEN GET THE VOTE

In sharp contrast to the methods of their English cousins, American women had been peacefully agitating for the right to vote since the days of Susan B. Anthony. In the twentieth century the movement spread, characterized by parades, picketings of the White House, and heckling of public men opposing the trend. By 1916 a dozen states had extended the franchise and both Presidential candidates declared themselves in favor. In 1919 Congress passed the Nineteenth Amendment which was proclaimed August 26, 1920, in time to allow women to vote in the Presidential election of that year.

THE POST-WAR DEPRESSION: 5,000,000 UNEMPLOYED

Soon after the war boom in industry a reaction set in, culminating in the depression of 1921. Wartime wages could not be maintained, and this tendency labor resisted strongly. Nation-wide strikes followed, especially in the railroad and coal industries. By 1921 there were more than 5,000,000 unemployed. However, by 1923 the country had begun the upswing which was to continue, almost uninterrupted, till 1929. The picture was taken in New York in 1922.

IMMIGRATION RESTRICTION: THE LAND OF PROMISE

The laws of 1921 and 1924 gave the United States a cohesive immigration policy at long last. Organized labor had long advocated restriction, but capital had opposed it, fearing it would bring high wages. The drastic reduction of 1921 was aimed at preventing exploitation of the country by unnaturalized aliens, and to hold back what threatened to be a flood of immigrants from the war-torn nations of Europe. But this law did not go far enough and in 1924 was passed the epoch-making act which fixed the annual quota of each nation at 2% of its immigrants to the United States in 1890. To all intents, the flood was shut off. The law superseded the "Gentlemen's Agreement" and infuriated Japan by excluding Asiatics. The photograph shows immigrants on Ellis Island in New York Harbor gazing toward "the land of promise."

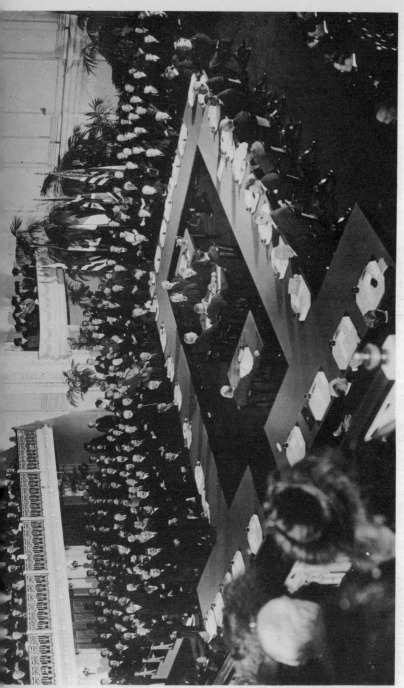

NAVAL DISARMAMENT CONFERENCE

Summoned by President Harding, delegates from eight European and Asiatic powers met at Washington on November 11, 1921, to discuss naval disarmament. A naval holiday of ten years was agreed upon and the tonnage of the three leading nations based on a 5:5:3 ratio for Great Britain, the United States, and Japan.

At the time the Conference seemed, and was so hailed throughout the world, as a great advance toward permanent peace. The treaty was rendered useless a decade later when Japan withdrew from the signatory nations, at a conference in London.

THE DAWES REPARATIONS COMMISSION

One of the controversial post-war problems was the matter of the war debts. At first, the British war debt to the United States was settled by an agreement spreading repayment of the amount owed over a long-term period. France, Italy, and Belgium, however, made their repayments contingent on Germany's paying indemnity to them. The constantly reiterated plaint of Germany that she could not pay led to the appointment by the Allied Reparation Commission of General Charles G. Dawes, Owen D. Young, and H. M. Robinson, below, to study the Reich's condition. The "Dawes Plan" was evolved whereby long-term payments of sums from earnings of German railroads and industries were coupled with a loan from the United States to assist the defeated country, and supervision of payments was placed in the hands of an American. Thus did the United States lend money to bankrupt Germany in the hope that she would pay the European allies, and that they would in turn pay America. The hope was realized to only a limited extent, for eventually another scheme, the Young Plan, had to be evolved, and finally came general European repudiation.

THE McNARY–HAUGEN BILLS

As a class the American farmer profited enormously during the war, by reason of the fact that the world was his market and the price he received for his products rose to unprecedented levels. With the early 1920's came the inevitable bursting of the bubble. Loth to accept virtually half of what he had become accustomed to, a "Farm Bloc" appeared in Congress which sought on his behalf to solve the question by national legislation. The McNary-Haugen bill providing for creation of a National Agricultural Export Commission with large capital resources to buy up farm surpluses and sell them abroad was passed in February, 1927, after three years' deliberation, but was vetoed by President Coolidge. A second bill in the next Congress to put the government into the farm business was also vetoed. Above, Senator Charles L. McNary, of Oregon, and Congressman Gilbert N. Haugen.

THE TEAPOT DOME SCANDALS

An outgrowth of the Harding administration was the scandal centering around Albert B. Fall, ex-Secretary of the Interior, which came as a result of his leasing naval oil reserve lands at Teapot Dome, Wyoming, and Elk Hills, California, to the Sinclair and Doheny interests. Fall had accepted a loan of $100,000 from Doheny without interest or security. Convicted of accepting a bribe, Fall was sentenced to a year's imprisonment. The Senate committee, of which Smoot and Lenroot were members, is shown above investigating the case which, in its ramifications, including that of jury-shadowing, dragged its sordid story through the courts for several years.

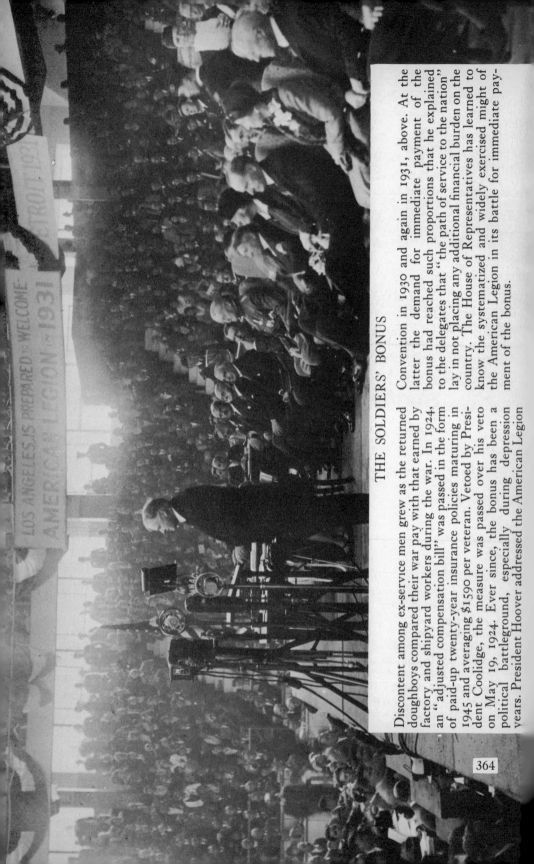

THE SOLDIERS' BONUS

Discontent among ex-service men grew as the returned doughboys compared their war pay with that earned by factory and shipyard workers during the war. In 1924, an "adjusted compensation bill" was passed in the form of paid-up twenty-year insurance policies maturing in 1945 and averaging $1590 per veteran. Vetoed by President Coolidge, the measure was passed over his veto on May 19, 1924. Ever since, the bonus has been a political battleground, especially during depression years. President Hoover addressed the American Legion Convention in 1930 and again in 1931, above. At the latter the demand for immediate payment of the bonus had reached such proportions that he explained to the delegates that "the path of service to the nation" lay in not placing any additional financial burden on the country. The House of Representatives has learned to know the systematized and widely exercised might of the American Legion in its battle for immediate payment of the bonus.

THE MARINES IN NICARAGUA ONCE MORE

Hardly had the Marines left Nicaragua in 1925 than that turbulent country was again in the throes of a revolution. The president and vice-president were exiled, but returned in 1926 to fight the régime of Adolfo Diaz, the Conservative incumbent. The United States furnished arms and munitions to the Diaz regime. In April, 1927, when the ex-president's army neared the capital, the United States compelled both factions to terminate hostilities. A guerilla warfare followed between the Marines and Sandino, an isolated rebel leader, whose forces were ultimately routed, but who remained uncaptured.

365

THE COMING OF RADIO

The daily habits of the nation were destined to be changed when the first commercial radio broadcast went on the air from Station KDKA, by employees of the Westinghouse Company at East Pittsburgh, in 1920. Music was furnished by phonograph records. The broadcast of the Dempsey-Carpentier fight in 1921 received only limited attention, but from 1921 to 1922 the new means of entertainment and news dissemination captured public attention and the country went radio-mad. Another industry, recreation, and educational influence had come into being. The picture shows an early experimental broadcasting station in the garage of Dr. Conrad's home in Pittsburgh.

THE GANGSTER ERA: CAPONE

Disrespect for the prohibition law reached a climax during the prosperous years. Outstanding among gangsters was "Scarface" Al Capone, whose illicit activities terrorized Chicago, and whose wealth enabled him to maintain the Florida mansion shown above. His skill in eluding direct responsibility, and at the same time enjoying his wealth, was illustrated when the Miami police tagged him for their Rogues' Gallery, yet could not jail him. Eventually he was convicted, not for the crimes which had terrorized Chicago, but for income-tax evasion—a federal offense.

THE NATION PROSPERS

From 1925 to 1929 the general prosperity of the country passed all records. Treasury surpluses were shown, despite slashing reductions in federal taxes and large payments on the national debt. Typical of the nation-wide enthusiasm was Chicago, which spread many millions of dollars over new tracts of land. In every American city new buildings rose, municipal improvements were made, and plans laid for a future that never arrived.

SIGNING THE KELLOGG–BRIAND PACT

On the tenth anniversary of the United States entry into the World War, the French Minister of Foreign Affairs, Aristide Briand, proposed both governments should sign a pact outlawing war and agreeing to settle all disputes pacifically. The pact was signed by Secretary of State Kellogg and President Coolidge January 17, 1928. Later Secretary Kellogg obtained the signatures of sixty-two nations to a similar proposal. The pact was to be flouted later by Japan's invasion of Manchuria.

COOLIDGE REFUSES TO RUN

In August, 1927, Calvin Coolidge, while on vacation in the West, announced, "I do not choose to run for President in 1928." The nation misjudged the strength of the determination that was behind this homely New England phraseology. Coolidge's administration was marked by continuing business prosperity and by his personal popularity, in great measure due to his refusal to embrace any idea not readily understood by the average man. The picture is typical of the many homely poses in which the President allowed himself to be photographed.

RACE RIOTS IN CHICAGO

In July, 1919, resentment at the moving of high-waged Negro workers into white residential districts in Chicago flared into a race riot. Both blacks and whites were killed. The rioting ended only after police and troops had removed the threatened families to safety. Above, white children cheering as a Negro's home is fired, and police removing one of the offenders to safety. Uprisings against Negro expansion also took place in other cities during this period.

WALL STREET EXPLOSION

At noon on a warm day in September, 1920, a drooping old horse drew a wagon into Wall Street and stopped before the United States Assay Office, across the street from J. P. Morgan & Company. An instant later there was a terrific explosion. Wall Street, from Nassau to William, was a shambles. Thirty-five were killed and more than a hundred injured. Direct responsibility for the tragedy, attributed to anti-capitalistic agitators, has never been definitely established.

372

KU KLUX KLAN: THE FIERY CROSS ABROAD AGAIN

Taking advantage of post-war emotionalism in the early 1920's, a group of Georgians revived the old Ku Klux Klan of the Civil War reconstruction period, and by modern publicity methods gained thousands of followers who were made to contribute heavily for the privilege of wearing the ghostly raiment of the Invisible Empire. Tarrings, featherings, floggings, and finally murders were attributed to the Klan's anti-Negro-Catholic-Jewish creed, and popular resentment and riots at Klan meetings followed. The movement spread throughout the eastern United States. Dissension broke out among its officials and the movement dwindled to isolated groups in remote districts.

373

THE ADVENT OF COOLIDGE

The illustration shows Calvin Coolidge entering the temporary executive quarters in the Senate Office Building as President, two days after Harding's death. While returning from a trip to Alaska, Harding had died at San Francisco on August 2, 1923. When Coolidge heard of his death he was visiting his boyhood home in Vermont. There, his father, a justice of the peace, by the light of an oil lamp in the parlor, swore his son in as Chief Executive. The dramatic quality of that scene in the New England farmhouse appealed to the traditional American feeling for things homely.

DESTRUCTION OF THE "SHENANDOAH"

Activities of the German Zeppelins in sea patrol service during the war prompted the Navy Department to undertake experiments in rigid airships. The *Los Angeles*, a non-combatant ship, was purchased from the Zeppelin Works, and made the transatlantic flight to the great naval hangar at Lakehurst, New Jersey. The first American rigid airship, the *Shenandoah*, was built at Akron, Ohio. After many successful flights, the craft was totally wrecked in an equinoctial storm over Ava, Ohio, September 3, 1925, its commander and thirteen others being killed.

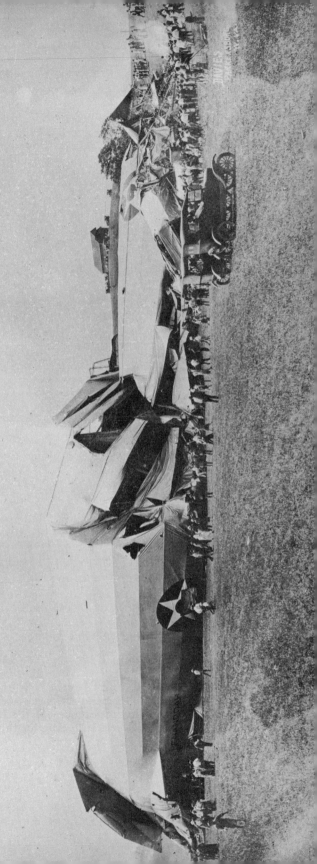

SINKING OF THE "S-51"

On the night of September 25, 1925, the submarine *S-51*, running on the surface off Block Island, was struck by the steamship *City of Rome*, sinking immediately. Three of the personnel were thrown off the deck as the doomed vessel plunged, and were rescued. Preliminary efforts to save those alive in the sunken craft proved unavailing and stormy winter seas prevented raising the wreck until the next year. The remainder of the crew, more than thirty men, were drowned in the submerged vessel. The photograph shows the first rescue ships trying to locate the lost submarine while a sister vessel stands by.

376

THE EUCHARISTIC CONGRESS IN CHICAGO

One of the most remarkable gatherings in the United States for a religious event took place during the Eucharistic Congress at Chicago, June, 1926, when Catholics from all over the country, to a number estimated at the time at 170,000, flocked to that city for a week of solemn observance. The Congress was accorded the honor of a Papal Legate, Cardinal Bonzano. Above is a view of Soldiers' Field with the high altar at the left where the Cardinal celebrated mass before the devout throng.

FIRST FLORIDA HURRICANE

Spurred by the example of Southern California, the state of Florida attracted thousands in a real estate boom in the early 1920's. The climate, accessibility by automobile, and public willingness to take a chance on liberal credit, led to gigantic developments. Miami quintupled her population between 1920 and 1925. On September 17–18, 1926, a West Indian hurricane struck Miami and the adjacent coast, wrecked the ornate Venetian residences, hurled ships and yachts into the streets, left a trail of 370 killed, and caused a property damage of $100,000,000. The Florida boom, one of the signs of the times, collapsed. Hardly over this first disaster, Florida experienced another hurricane on almost the same date in 1928. Many times more persons were killed by it, but the property damage was much less.

THE MISSISSIPPI FLOODS

Starting in 1926, torrential rainstorms in Kansas, Arkansas and Missouri, breaking all previous records. eastern Oklahoma, and the Ohio Valley brought flooded New Orleans was only saved by dynamiting the levee conditions in those sections which occasioned little below the city. The Red Cross undertook relief to the national alarm. But in April, 1927, came floods of gigan- thousands of homeless, and the nation contributed tic proportions in the Mississippi Valley, especially in generally.

379

THE SACCO-VANZETTI CASE

Fear that Bolshevist doctrines might spread from Russia to the United States, coupled with increased activities of Communists and other radicals, threw the country into a "Red" scare during the post-war period. The sentencing to death of two Italian anarchists for the murder of a paymaster and his guard at South Braintree, Massachusetts, focused world attention on the situation. The radical press at home and abroad was loud in its denunciation of American justice. Governor Fuller and a board of review, however, were adamant, and the two men were electrocuted on August 23, 1927, after several years of ineffectual agitation for their release.

THE PRIZE RING LOSES ITS STIGMA

Frowned on in the Nineteenth Century, pugilism became a national fetish
after the war. The great throngs, representing all walks of life, that came to
see the fights were indicative of a country casting off old bonds and reveling
in unprecedented prosperity. Outstanding in the era was the return fight
between Gene Tunney, heavyweight champion, and Jack Dempsey, former
champion, at Chicago, on September 22, 1927, when almost 150,000 people
crowded into Soldiers' Field to see the battle. The illustration shows the
famous "Long Count" when Tunney, floored, had more than the usual ten-
second interval in which to rise, due to Dempsey's slowness in going to the
corner of the ring.

SINKING OF THE "S-4"

During the Prohibition era, the Coast Guard was allotted a number of obsolete destroyers to aid in capturing rum-running ships off the coasts. One of them accidentally ran down the submarine *S-4* off Provincetown, December 17, 1927, the entire crew of 40 being lost. Divers located the sunken craft and for hours those living of the crew tapped out code messages on the hull, but rescue efforts were impossible, due to heavy weather. It is interesting to remember, as a mark of the times, that the "wets" seized on this tragedy to further the cause of Prohibition reform. The vessel is shown after she was raised and brought to Boston.

SINKING OF THE "VESTRIS"

On November 12, 1928, the British steamship *Vestris*, bound from New York to Barbadoes, Rio de Janeiro, and Buenos Aires, ran into a heavy storm off the Virginia Capes and sustained such damage that it sank, carrying down one hundred and ten passengers and crew. In the investigation that followed charges were made that the ship had been allowed to sail from New York with its cargo improperly loaded, causing a heavy list. Others attributed it to damage caused by a hurricane. The picture is one of the most remarkable views of a marine disaster ever photographed.

REPRINTED BY COURTESY OF THE NEW YORK "NEWS."

INAUGURATION OF THE AIR MAIL SERVICE

The United States showed the same slowness in carrying the mail by air, despite years of such transportation abroad, that it had in recognizing the epoch-making invention of the Wright brothers. It was not until May 15, 1918, that the first air mail service was begun, a comparatively short "hop," between New York and Washington. Below is shown President Wilson greeting the pioneer pilot at Potomac Field. The flight ushered in the development of the modern air service.

384

FLIGHT OF THE "NC-4" ACROSS THE ATLANTIC

With a string of warships stationed at intervals along their route in case of trouble, the Navy flying-boats NC-1, NC-3, and NC-4 left Rockaway Beach, New York, May 8, 1919, in an attempt to cross the Atlantic by airplane. They reached Trepassey Bay, Newfoundland, and on May 16th headed for the Azores. Of the three, only the NC-4 made the journey by air, the time being a little more than 15 hours. The NC-1 was forced down and sank, a steamer rescuing the crew. The NC-3 also suffered a mishap, but navigated on the surface to Ponta Delgada safely. The NC-4 afterward flew to Spain and England. Crossing the ocean in heavier-than-air machines had been proved feasible. The photograph shows the start of the three planes from Rockaway Beach.

END OF THE FIRST NON–STOP ATLANTIC FLIGHT

Early transatlantic flights by American aviators often obscure the fact that to Britain belongs the credit for the first non-stop transatlantic airplane journey. On June 14–15, 1919, eight years before Lindbergh's achievement, John Alcock and Arthur W. Brown flew their Vickers-Vimy biplane, similar to a wartime bomber, from St. Johns, Newfoundland, to Clifden, Ireland, in safety. The plane sustained damage in landing, as the pilot brought it down in an Irish bog, but 1960 miles had been flown in a little more than 16 hours.

AROUND THE WORLD BY AIR

Though the Navy made the first transatlantic airplane flight, the Army did its part in a round-the-world flight that made history. Four Douglas biplanes started from Santa Monica, California, March 17, 1924, and headed for Seattle, the official starting point. One plane was forced down in Alaska. The remaining three continued on the trip but one of them was wrecked in attempting to reach Iceland, after Asia and Europe had been successfully spanned. Lieutenants Smith and Nelson piloted the remaining two to Seattle, where they landed on September 28th. The photograph shows the welcoming crowd at Mitchel Field, Long Island, N. Y., one of the stops made near the end of the flight.

BYRD FLIES OVER THE NORTH POLE

Another flying achievement was credited to America when Commander Richard E. Byrd and Floyd Bennett, U. S. Navy, took off from King's Bay, near Spitzbergen, on May 9, 1926, and reached the North Pole. They circled it successfully and returned, having covered 1500 miles over the Arctic wastes. Their trip was of geographic value for it showed no new land in the area over which they traveled. The picture shows the Byrd plane returning to Spitzbergen from the flight over the Pole.

LINDBERGH'S FLIGHT TO PARIS

The aviation event which most captured popular fancy in the pioneer years of transatlantic flight was the solo trip of Charles A. Lindbergh from New York to Paris in his Ryan monoplane *Spirit of St. Louis*. He hopped off while more pretentious expeditions were in course of preparation, in the early hours of May 20, 1927. Al-though he encountered bad weather, he landed his craft at Paris, 3610 miles away, in 33 hours and 29 minutes. Above, the landing at Le Bourget airdrome near Paris, with soldiers and gendarmes holding back a wildly enthusiastic crowd.

LINDBERGH REACHES HOME

A Twentieth Century version of a Roman triumph was accorded the modest hero when he arrived in New York from Washington, June 13, 1927. Not the least of the honors accorded him was the fact that a United States warship, the *Memphis*, was sent to bring this private citizen home. Niagaras of ticker tape and torn paper fluttered into the streets as he passed, amidst the cheers of hundreds of thousands. It was the height of prosperity, and the city's greeting was extended by the then popular Mayor, James J. Walker.

BYRD'S FLIGHT TO FRANCE

On June 29th, not long after Lindbergh's triumph, Commander Byrd left New York for France in the giant monoplane "America," with his crack pilot, Bernt Balchen, and an experienced crew. They arrived over France in a fog at night and for hours circled about, completely lost. A fast-disappearing gasoline supply forced a landing on the stony beach of Ver-sur-Mer, a tiny village, the plane being badly damaged. Between the Lindbergh flight and the Byrd flight, Clarence Chamberlin had piloted Charles Levine from New York to Germany, covering almost 4000 miles non-stop. These three flights roused the country, as nothing else could have done, to the tremendous strides made in aviation since the war.

THE PANIC OF OCTOBER, 1929

The Belshazzar's Feast of American prosperity was not without some handwriting on the wall. Certain conservative economists had warned against such an orgy of optimism, but it was not until October, 1929, that their warnings were heeded. The Stock Market collapsed, and a stampede to sell stocks set in, 12,800,000 shares being sold October 24th, and 16,400,000 shares October 29th. Fortunes vanished, paper profits were wiped out, and gilt-edged securities sank to record lows. The picture shows the crowd in front of the Stock Exchange during the panic. In the wake of the crash came unemployment, idle factories, bank failures, foreclosures, and falling off in prices generally.

BANK FAILURES

One of the first effects on the nation's financial structure, as the depression deepened, was a wave of bank closings, the like of which had never been experienced. It showed the inherent weakness of many of the state banking laws. A notable failure was that of The Bank of the United States, in New York, in December, 1930. It seems probable that the name of the bank induced many ignorant people to deposit their money therein. A crowd is shown in front of one of the institution's many branches.

THE HOOVER MORATORIUM

Not only the United States but virtually the entire world had been sliding down the depression incline for almost two years when President Hoover, in an effort to relieve one of the international difficulties, proposed in June, 1931, a one-year moratorium on payments of all inter-governmental war debts and conditional reparations. The proposal was approved with modifications by France, and later by other interested nations. Undoubtedly the moratorium eased the situation somewhat, but it did not cure the cycle of bad business which had yet to run its complete course. The picture shows Secretary of the Treasury Mellon and Ambassador Edge leaving the Quai d'Orsay in Paris after France had signed the moratorium.

THE RECONSTRUCTION FINANCE CORPORATION

President Hoover sought to halt the depression by asking business not to interrupt its expansion program or reduce wages, by appointing a Cabinet committee to investigate means of reducing unemployment, and by planning for public works, farm relief, and emergency construction. In early 1932, he created the Reconstruction Finance Corporation, with a capital of $2,000,000,000, to make loans to railroads, insurance companies, agricultural associations, banks, and other enterprises. The directors of the corporation, including Charles G. Dawes, who had just resigned as ambassador to Great Britain, are shown above.

THE BONUS ARMY

Several thousand unemployed veterans, at the height of the depression in the spring of 1932, converged on Washington and camped on Government property, demanding immediate payment of the soldier's bonus, not due until 1945. The Washington police, after temporizing, ordered them to move out of the city, and when they refused attempted to evict them. The veterans beat the police off, and troops were called out who routed the malcontents with tear gas and tanks. President Hoover was charged with using American soldiers against impoverished patriots, and the accusation lost him many votes in the November election in which he was defeated for re-election.

396

END OF AN ERA: MAYOR WALKER

Throughout the depression there became manifest a desire to be rid of established political orders, whether Democratic or Republican. This was especially in evidence in cities where municipal finance was beginning to be called to account for maladministration and graft. In New York in 1932 the once popular Mayor and play-boy, James J. Walker, proved vulnerable to attack. Eventually he resigned under fire and left the country.

INSULL: A FIGURE OF THE TIMES

Prior to 1929, despite the anti-trust laws, vast holding corporations grew throughout the country, embracing many major industries. Sale of their shares was widespread, due to popular faith in their future, and certain economic benefits derived from standardization and elimination of waste methods among their subsidiaries. With the stock-market crash, the popular dream vanished and a wave of resentment swept over the country against those who promoted the ambitious schemes. Typical was the case of Samuel Insull, Mid-West utilities magnate, who fled to Europe to escape prosecution, was extradited after a long pursuit, and subsequently acquitted. The picture shows Insull at the Chicago Century of Progress Exposition.

398

END OF THE NICARAGUAN ADVENTURE

With growing agitation in Congress for their removal and a certain amount of equilibrium attained in the Nicaraguan government, the Marines evacuated that country in January, 1933. Sandino, the rebel leader, whom the sea-soldiers had failed to catch, though they killed many of his followers, at once made peace with President Sacasa but was later kidnaped and murdered. Thus was ended another attempt by the United States to protect its South American interests by force. The picture shows the arrival of the Marines at Quantico in January.

ROOSEVELT INAUGURATED

Herbert Hoover went down to defeat in November, 1932, before an electorate which charged the Republican party for much of the depression and him personally for failure to cure it. The New Deal arrived March 4, 1933, when Franklin Delano Roosevelt was inaugurated. As with Lincoln, his term began during a national crisis with the added burden that 12,000,000 were unemployed throughout the land. The country was in the midst of a banking panic which the Republicans have since claimed might have been averted had the incoming President not refused to coöperate in efforts to stem it. With every bank in the country closed, general panic was averted by Roosevelt's use of the radio to carry into American homes his assurance that the banks would reopen shortly, and a new phase of national life would be entered that would lead out of the economic quagmire.

400

"BRAIN TRUST"

Shortly after his inauguration, President Roosevelt surrounded himself with a group of confidential advisers, most of them not cabinet members. Some of this group were college professors and the public quickly named the advisers the "Brain Trust." Big business severely criticized the President's action in listening to the theories of men whom industrial leaders believed to be theorists and visionaries. The personnel of the "Brain

Trust," underwent changes as the Administration progressed, but the group itself was maintained in the face of much adverse comment. The picture shows Roosevelt, as President-Elect, conferring with Raymond Moley, chief "brain truster," and, until shortly before, of the faculty of Columbia University, at Hyde Park, New York.

GOLD STANDARD ABANDONED

On April 19, 1933, President Roosevelt ordered an embargo on all gold exports, thus officially taking the country off the international gold standard. Earlier in the month he had prohibited the hoarding of gold, while at the time of his temporary closing of the banks he had prohibited the withdrawal of gold or silver for domestic or export trade. Congress validated the President's actions, and invested him with monetary powers to use at his discretion. Above, under heavy guard and at night, gold valued at $750,000,000 being removed from the San Francisco Mint for shipment to Denver.

THE F. E. R. A.: 14,000,000 UNEMPLOYED

The number of men out of work throughout the country reached an all-time high in March, 1933, with about 14,000,000 jobless. An effort was made through the Federal Emergency Relief Administration, in coöperation with the states, to relieve the hardships of these stricken people and their families. Many unemployed, thousands of whom were homeless, established "shanty-towns" on vacant lots in cities, building shacks from cast-off material. The situation was without precedent in the nation's history.

403

BEER RETURNS

One of the first results of the administration of Franklin D. Roosevelt was the legalization of 3.2 per cent beer. The cry, in part, was that this would raise large revenues and put men to work, but the fact was that the nation wanted an end of prohibition. The appearance of trucks hauling the now-legalized beverages never failed to create interest. Some few horse-drawn trucks went into service just as in "the good old days," but they were mostly for purposes of atmosphere. Many states, foreseeing the end of prohibition, took steps at this early stage to prevent the return of the old-time saloon.

404

THE CENTURY OF PROGRESS

In the face of the most stringent period, the city of Chicago sounded a note of national optimism with its "Century of Progress" exposition, held in 1933. The great Fair, constructed on artificially made land on the shores of Lake Michigan, glorified the achievements of the Machine Age with buildings expressing the new note in architecture. In contrast to other attempts, immediately previous, to hold "world's fairs," the Chicago venture was a financial success and was repeated the following summer.

COMING OF THE N. R. A.

One of Roosevelt's efforts to end the depression was the National Industrial Recovery Act, which he sponsored, authorizing the President to establish agencies to assist in bringing about recovery. One of these was the National Recovery Administration, which set about placing industry under codes, fixing maximum work weeks, minimum rates of pay, eliminating destructive price competition, and aiming toward establishment of fair business methods. Firms complying with the codes were given the right to display a "Blue Eagle" insignia. The movement was ushered in by parades in many cities, such as the New York one above, showing support of the plan. The fiery General Hugh Johnson as head of the N. R. A. Board soon began taking to himself much of the limelight in Washington.

THE FARM STRIKE

In the Northwest and Middle West the farm situation in 1933 was as bad as that of unemployment in the industrial areas. Unable to obtain even production cost prices for their commodities, farmers in several states staged a form of strike, picketed roads into cities and destroyed truckloads of milk and produce attempting to reach the markets. The movement was broken up by state troops and increased Governmental attention to farm relief.

SOVIET RUSSIA RECOGNIZED

Correspondence between Washington and the U.S.S.R. was made public before the end of President Roosevelt's first year in office, showing that the way was being paved for formal recognition of the existing Russian government. On November 16, 1933, recognition took place, the Soviet government binding itself to refrain from interfering in this country's internal affairs and guaranteeing American rights and religious freedom in Russia. Above is shown United States Ambassador William C. Bullitt arriving in Moscow.

THE C.C.C.: CARING FOR JOBLESS YOUTH

To alleviate the plight of thousands of young men out of work, or unable to obtain jobs on leaving school, the Civilian Conservation Corps was created by act of Congress, providing for enlistments at nominal pay for engaging in work of reforestation, flood control, soil erosion protection, and other activities. Money was set aside to finance the conservation work, and by the spring of 1933 thousands of these young men were engaged in the healthful work. The idea of the camps is said to have been President Roosevelt's. In any case it was one of the early triumphs of the "New Deal." The photograph shows the President visiting one of the camps.

REPEAL OF PROHIBITION

"The noble experiment" approached its end when the Lame Duck session of Congress, February 16 and 20, 1933, passed the Twenty-first Amendment to the Constitution, repealing the Eighteenth. The nation responded quickly to the opportunity to express its opinion on a law that could not have been and never was enforced. By December, Prohibition was in the past. When the Utah state Senate ratified repeal and thereby wrote "Finis" to an era which had resulted in widespread disrespect for law and the development of a new criminal class, legal liquor again began to flow across the nation's bars amid scenes of genuine and, on the whole, restrained celebration.

THE NEW DEAL REACHES CONGRESS

At the opening of Congress in January, 1934, President Roosevelt placed before it his program for the "New Deal." It called for reorganization of the political and economic system so that the Government would thereafter take an active part in coöperating with business to bring about national stability. The President's outline covered three phases—relief, "reflation," and reform.

THE A. A. A. AND THE FARMER

The Agricultural Adjustment Administration was another of the major measures instituted by the New Deal. It concentrated on restriction of acreage and production of agricultural commodities in order to provide increased agricultural purchasing power, orderly liquidation of joint-stock land banks, and other results beneficial to the farmer. It was instituted in May, 1933. At that time farm mortgages were being foreclosed; and commodity prices were about 50 per cent of those before the war.

THE P. W. A.: A HOUSING PROJECT

The Public Works Administration was another channel through which the administration struck at the depression. It was allotted $3,300,000,000, partly in grants, partly in loans, to be spent on public works, either Federal or of community benefit, and gave employment to thousands otherwise idle. A typical example of its accomplishments is shown above in the gigantic housing project completed in the Bronx section of New York City, to accommodate families at low rents in comfortable, healthful apartments.

DROUGHT IN THE WEST

Early in the spring of 1934 a drought appeared in the Northwest and spread rapidly to the Southeast, South, and Southwest. By the end of May it had developed into the worst on record. The feed and forage shortage resulted in the deaths of many thousands of livestock, and wrought untold misery on the farmers, until the arrival of benefit payments in the crop adjustment program and the wholesale purchase of drought-cattle stocks by the AAA somewhat alleviated the situation.

THE SAN FRANCISCO GENERAL STRIKE

One phenomenon that set off the depression years from similar previous periods was the absence of a series of widespread and prolonged strikes, with inevitable violence, bloodshed, and death, following in their wake. This does not mean that such strikes as there were, were not serious. The most widespread was the general strike in San Francisco in the summer of 1934. The photograph shows a protest mass meeting in the Civil Center during the height of the strike.

THE N. R. A. DECISION

While the Administration was contending for extension of the N. R. A. the Supreme Court on May 27, 1935, rendered a unanimous decision declaring the act to be unconstitutional, asserting that it unlawfully delegated to others authority vested in Congress and that as applied to intrastate operation it usurped power belonging to the states. The decision upset a primary essential of the New Deal program, nullifying all industrial codes then in effect. Donald Richberg, Chairman of the Industrial Recovery Board, is shown on May 20th before the House Ways and Means Committee, pleading for the long-term continuance of the N. R. A. Act.

BYRD FLIES OVER THE SOUTH POLE

In 1929, Commander Richard E. Byrd set out for a year in the Antarctic, with the most completely equipped exploring expedition in history. Establishing a base at Little America, on the edge of the Antarctic, the expedition assembled a great Ford monoplane, the *Floyd Bennett*, named after the pilot who had flown with Byrd to the North Pole. On November 28th the plane took off and in 19 hours made the trip to the southern tip of the earth, where it circled the Pole, dropped flags of the United States and England, and returned to Little America. The picture shows Byrd preparing to take off for the flight.

THE POST–GATTY WORLD FLIGHT

Jules Verne's fictional world tour in eighty days was reduced ninety per cent by aviation when Wiley Post and Harold Gatty flew their monoplane *Winnie Mae* from New York in late June, 1931, on a record-breaking trip by way of England, Germany, Russia, Siberia, Alaska, Canada, and to their home port, their time for the journey being eight days, fifteen hours, fifty-one minutes. Depression New York was not too depressed to give the aviators a rousing reception. The above shows Post climbing out of the cockpit at the end of the flight. He later became notable in the field of stratosphere flying. On August 15, 1935, he and the much-beloved humorist and motion-picture star, Will Rogers, met death while on an aërial holiday in Alaska.

418

LOSS OF THE "AKRON"

The disaster to the *Shenandoah* did not deter the Navy from its experiments with rigid airships, and the *Akron* was built and flown for thousands of miles. The success of the ship was short-lived, for on April 4, 1933, it ran into an electrical storm off the New Jersey coast and was totally destroyed. Rear Admiral Moffett, naval aeronautics chief, and almost all of the crew, perished. The illustration shows the port fin of the dirigible being salvaged from the depths.

ARMY AIR MAIL DISASTERS

In February, 1934, the Administration suddenly cancelled all air mail contracts, alleging there had been "fraud and collusion" in letting them. A protest went up from all the commercial companies, and even Colonel Lindbergh characterized such action as condemnation without a trial. The Army was ordered to fly the mail. By the end of March eleven army pilots had crashed to their deaths. The army planes were not equipped nor the pilots trained for this type of service. The weather in late February and March was bad but no worse than that flown in previous years by the commercial lines. Ultimately new contracts were let with commercial lines.

SETTLE–FORDNEY STRATOSPHERE FLIGHT

On the morning of November 20, 1933, Lt.-Commander T. G. M. Settle and Major C. L. Fordney stepped into the globular gondola of their stratosphere balloon at Akron, Ohio, and amid cheers soared aloft. Ascending 61,243 feet, or more than eleven and a half miles, they reached an unprecedented altitude. From that height the balloon drifted to Bayside, Long Island, where a successful landing was made in a swamp. Aside from the spectacular nature of the flight, considerable valuable scientific data was obtained.

OHIO STATE PENITENTIARY FIRE

One night in April, 1930, fire and rioting broke out in the Ohio State Penitentiary at Columbus under circumstances that indicated an attempt at a wholesale jail delivery. State and Federal troops rushed to the scene and cowed the rioting, but not before the fire had engulfed four cell blocks, resulting in the deaths of more than three hundred prisoners. It was among the worst prison fires on record, and the most serious of several prison outbreaks in recent years. The photograph shows a scene outside the prison in the early morning hours.

GEORGE WASHINGTON BRIDGE

One of the outstanding engineering feats of the world was the building of
the George Washington suspension bridge over the Hudson River above
New York City. The channel span, measuring 3500 feet, will remain the
longest in the world until the new one across the Golden Gate at San Francisco is completed. It was a far cry from this monster with its speeding
automobiles to the crowds rioting on the Brooklyn Bridge for fear it would
fall. The photograph shows the bridge on opening day in October, 1931.

LINDBERGH KIDNAPING

While on a "goodwill" flight to Mexico, Lindbergh met, and some time after married, the daughter of Ambassador Dwight W. Morrow. On the night of March 1, 1932, the entire world was horrified by the kidnaping of their baby son from their home (white spot at extreme upper right of picture), at Hopewell, New Jersey (group of buildings just above center). On May 12th, the decomposed body of the child was discovered in the woods (note automobiles parked on the road as it skirts the woods, left center), four miles from their home. For the next three years kidnaping became America's worst "racket," one sensational case following another. Public feeling eventually made possible the "Lindbergh Law," under which kidnaping, given certain circumstances, became a federal offense, punishable by death.

424

THE OLYMPIC GAMES

For the first time in history the Olympic Games were held in America in 1932. With impressive ceremonies Vice-President Charles Curtis opened the Olympiad in Los Angeles in an especially constructed stadium. Out of seventeen records established in the men's track and field events nine were made by United States entries. Most sensational were the victories in the 100-meter and 200-meter runs of the great Negro sprinter "Eddie" Tolan.

425

ATTEMPT ON ROOSEVELT'S LIFE

President-elect Roosevelt was in Miami on the night of February 15, 1933. The picture shows him as he waved to the welcoming crowd. A few seconds later, Joseph Zangara, a half-crazed person, fired at him, missing, but hitting Mayor Anton Cermak, of Chicago, who later died of the wound. Zangara paid for his crime with his life. The nation breathed relief at Roosevelt's escape for, aside from the horror of the crime itself, it was looking to him personally to lead the country out of the depression.

SAN JOSE LYNCHING

Mob murder has not infrequently been one of the darker sides of American life. Outstanding mob action in 1933 was the lynching of two confessed kidnap-slayers at San José, California, in November. The lynchers are shown below battering their way into the jail. The Governor of California's announcement that he would make no move to hunt down those responsible for the outrage, called forth widespread denunciation, despite the fact that the victims were suspected of having committed a particularly brutal murder in addition to the crime of kidnaping.

427

NAVAL REVIEW

In May, 1934, for the first time, the main fleet of the United States Navy passed through the Panama Canal from the Pacific to the Atlantic and proceeded northward to New York, where President Roosevelt, himself an enthusiastic sailor, and former Assistant Secretary of the Navy, reviewed it from the cruiser *Indianapolis* off Ambrose Light. It was the greatest concentration of American naval strength ever held.

END OF AN ERA: DILLINGER'S LAST RIDE

In 1933 and 1934, in an effort to stem a tide of vicious but isolated crimes, the Federal government extended the police powers of its agents, and the "G" men commenced a war with gangdom. The turn of the tide came when John Dillinger, outstanding jail-breaker, bank-robber, and murderer, was cornered coming out of a Chicago theater, on July 22, 1934, and shot down by the Federal men. In the months following, the Federal agents, under the power given them, commenced to gain the upper hand. The era of the gangster was passing.

BURNING OF THE "MORRO CASTLE"

A marine disaster that led to revelations of laxness in the enforcement of the rules of safety at sea occurred when the Ward liner *Morro Castle* burned off the Jersey coast with a great loss of life, especially among the passenger list. Fire of unknown origin broke out in the writing-room on the night of September 8, 1934, and swept the ship. Many were trapped in their berths, others leaping into the sea to escape the flames, only to drown. The Federal Steamboat Inspection Service later held a number of the officers of the ship on charges of negligence in spreading the alarm and combating the fire. The photograph shows the gutted ship on the sand at Asbury Park where she was beached.

THE HAUPTMANN TRIAL

In September, 1934, two gasoline station attendants in the Bronx noticed
a customer who paid them with a gold treasury note, then forbidden by
Federal ruling. The result of their vigilance was the arrest of a German
ex-convict, Bruno Richard Hauptmann, a Bronx carpenter, for the kidnaping and murder of the Lindbergh baby. Search of Hauptmann and his home
resulted in the finding of $15,000 of the Lindbergh baby's ransom money,
which had been paid by Colonel Lindbergh to the kidnaper, in a futile
effort to regain the child. Placed on trial at Flemington, New Jersey, he was
convicted and sentenced to death, in February, 1935.

GEORGE WASHINGTON

1732–1799, PRESIDENT, 1789–1797

"If you speak of solid information and sound judgment," said Patrick Henry at the First Continental Congress, "Colonel Washington is unquestionably the greatest man on the floor." Unanimously elected Commander-in-Chief of the Revolutionary forces, Washington led them to victory and was afterwards unanimously elected President of the new nation. The so-called Presidents who came before him —there were nine, including John Hancock who did not serve—presided over the Continental Congresses. Washington was the first President under the Constitution. His first inauguration took place at the old Federal Hall on Wall Street, New York City, April 30, 1789.

JOHN ADAMS

1735–1826, PRESIDENT, 1797–1801

John Adams, the first Vice-President, was inaugurated President on March 4, 1797, in Philadelphia where Washington's second inauguration took place. According to the Constitution as it then existed the candidate receiving the second highest number of electoral votes automatically became Vice-President. This gave the office to Thomas Jefferson, a man whose political faith was exactly the opposite of that of the President, the former preaching the sovereignty of the people while the latter fought for a "government by an aristocracy of talents and wealth." The Constitution was amended in 1804 to provide separate ballots for Vice-President. Adams was the first President to live in the White House.

432

JAMES MADISON

1751–1836, PRESIDENT, 1809–1817

Rightly called the "Father of the Constitution," the fourth President was one of the ablest men of his day, but he lacked the gift of winning the affection of the people he served. Socially speaking, his greatest asset was his wife, "Dolly" Madison who in 1801 when her husband was Secretary of State became official hostess for the widowed President Jefferson and for sixteen years filled the position of "First Lady of the Land" with unprecedented grace and charm. The country is still indebted to her for saving the valuable state papers which she carried with her in 1814 when she was obliged to flee before the British invasion of Washington.

433

THOMAS JEFFERSON

1743–1826, PRESIDENT, 1801–1809

Before his death the Sage of Monticello wrote an inscription for his tomb setting forth what he felt were his three chief claims to remembrance: "Here was buried Thomas Jefferson, author of the Declaration of American Independence, of the Statute of Virginia for Religious Freedom, and Father of the University of Virginia." To these should be added "Negotiator of the Louisiana Purchase, Founder of the Democratic party." Jefferson died on July 4, 1826, fifty years after the signing of the Declaration of Independence. His old friend and rival, John Adams, died the same day. Adams' last words were, "Jefferson still survives."

JAMES MONROE

1758–1831, PRESIDENT, 1817–1825

Harmony followed the close of the War of 1812 and the eight years of Monroe's administration are still cited as the "era of good feeling." So great was the President's popularity he would have been unanimously elected for his second term except that a delegate from New Hampshire, deeming only Washington worthy of such honor, cast a prophetic vote for John Quincy Adams. It was a time of expansion and prosperity. Five states were admitted to the Union, Florida was purchased from Spain and Europe was warned (Monroe Doctrine) to keep hands off American and Pan-American affairs. Even the question of slavery was momentarily settled by the Missouri Compromise of 1820.

JOHN QUINCY ADAMS

1767–1848, PRESIDENT, 1825–1829

Son of the second President, John Quincy Adams was elected to office in one of the bitterest campaigns ever waged in this country. The Fathers of the Revolution were too old to serve, and for the first time the Republic had to look to a new generation for leadership. Five candidates were offered: Adams of Massachusetts, Andrew Jackson of Tennessee, Henry Clay of Kentucky, William H. Crawford of Georgia, and John C. Calhoun of South Carolina. Calhoun withdrew before the election. None of the others received a majority and when the House of Representatives had to make the final choice from among the three with the highest number Adams was selected. Like his father, he served only one term.

434

MARTIN VAN BUREN

1782–1862, PRESIDENT, 1837–1841

The eighth President was the first natural-born citizen of the Republic to become Chief Executive. The Republic was six years old when he was born. Van Buren was an adroit politician, long a leader of the notorious Albany Regency which controlled the politics of New York State. He was the first President of Dutch ancestry, and like the two others, the Roosevelts, who were also New Yorkers, he served as Governor of his State before he became President. He failed to win a second term. The country was in the grip of its first great financial crisis and the conservative Whigs were determined to break down the Jackson-Van Buren machine.

ANDREW JACKSON

1767–1845, PRESIDENT, 1829–1837

Son of the frontier, hero of the Battle of New Orleans and the Indian Wars, "Old Hickory" was the first man of the common people to become President. All his predecessors were aristocrats, all men of property, and all except Washington college graduates. Jackson was the first President to build up a party machine, and with the "spoils system," the first to introduce patronage into national politics. He was enthusiastically re-elected on a platform to take the government away from the "money power" and he was one of the few Presidents to leave office with a larger following than he had at the time of his inauguration.

435

WILLIAM HENRY HARRISON

1773–1841, PRESIDENT, MARCH 4–APRIL 4, 1841

The Whigs selected General William Henry ("Tippecanoe") Harrison, an old hero of the Indian wars, as their candidate in 1840, and, taking a leaf from the book of the Democrats, rushed him into office with a campaign emphasizing his homespun virtues and simplicity in contrast with the supposedly luxurious lives of such Democrats as Van Buren. This was the famous "log cabin and cider" campaign, so called because the General was born in a log cabin and served cider at his table instead of wine. The tumult and the shouting were too much for the old man. He died on April 4, 1841, one month after his inauguration.

JOHN TYLER

1790–1862, PRESIDENT, 1841–1845

The tenth President was the first of the "accidental Presidents," that is, the first to reach office by way of the Vice-Presidency. He was a Democrat, nominated by the Whigs to catch the votes of his party. "Tippecanoe and Tyler too" had been the slogan of the campaign, but the Whigs never intended Tyler for the Presidency. He lacked party support and was able to accomplish little. Long before the end of his term he and the Whigs were at odds and he was not reëlected. In 1861 he was made a member of the Confederate Congress but died in Richmond before he had a chance to serve.

436

ZACHARY TAYLOR

1784–1850, PRESIDENT, 1849–JULY 9, 1850

For forty years a soldier, with a term of service extending from the War of 1812 to the War with Mexico, General Zachary Taylor came to the Presidency without previous political experience of any kind. The Whigs nominated him because they had learned that the easiest way to beat the Democrats was to select a popular military figure; after the War with Mexico "Old Rough and Ready" was the best qualified man in the country in this respect. What kind of President he might have made was never learned, for he never had a chance to prove himself. He died suddenly on July 9, 1850, sixteen months after his inauguration.

JAMES KNOX POLK

1795–1849, PRESIDENT, 1845–1849

In 1844 the Whigs ran Henry Clay against a young lawyer from Tennessee, one James K. Polk (originally Pollock), and lost the election. Polk's administration was notable for the acquisition of Texas, California, and New Mexico through the War with Mexico and for the final settlement of the boundary dispute with Great Britain over the limits of the Oregon Territory. Polk declared himself for the masses and condemned the Whigs and Federalists for trying to transfer money "from the pockets of the people to the favored classes." It is interesting to note in the light of later developments that Mrs. Polk banished dancing and drink from the White House.

437

MILLARD FILLMORE

1800–1874, PRESIDENT, 1850–1853

The thirteenth President was a man of many virtues who would probably have never reached national distinction except for the accident of General Taylor's death which raised him from the Vice-Presidency to the highest office in the land. He was an earnest, self-made man, a lawyer, "eminent for his calm and pacific temperament." He wrecked his political career in 1852 when he signed the Fugitive Slave Law providing for the surrender of runaway slaves. In 1856 he was nominated for the Presidency by the Know Nothings, but gained the electorai vote of only one state. The last twenty years of his life were spent in Buffalo, New York.

FRANKLIN PIERCE

1804–1869, PRESIDENT, 1853–1857

The Whig formula for winning the Presidency with a military candidate met defeat in 1852 when Franklin Pierce, a New Hampshire Democrat, won a smashing victory over General Winfield Scott with a platform advocating slavery and tariff for revenue only. The Whig party did not survive the disaster; the next campaign was fought between the newly organized Republicans and the Democrats. Pierce selected an able Cabinet, including men of all factions, Northern and Southern Democrats, anti-slavery Northerners, a Massachusetts Whig, and an ardent states rights Southerner, Jefferson Davis. It was one of the few Cabinets which has remained unchanged throughout an administration.

438

ABRAHAM LINCOLN

1809–1865, PRESIDENT, 1861–1865

"A homely hero born of star and sod," the son of Thomas Lincoln and Nancy Hanks was at the beginning of his career dismissed as "an ignorant Western boor," yet he alone among the Presidents holds today an unquestioned position at the side of George Washington. His tragic death on April 15, 1865, at the hands of John Wilkes Booth added a martyr's crown to his glories, but his place among the immortals was already secure. The feeling of the people is truly recorded in the inscription behind the Lincoln statue in the great Lincoln Memorial in Washington: "In this temple as in the hearts of the people for whom he saved the Union the memory of Abraham Lincoln is enshrined forever."

439

JAMES BUCHANAN

1791–1868, PRESIDENT, 1857–1861

Having won distinction in both Houses of Congress, as a diplomatic representative, and as Secretary of State under Polk, the fifteenth President, a Democrat, came into office during the troubled years preceding the Civil War. "They tell me," he said, "that the use of my name will still the agitated waters, restore public harmony by banishing sectionalism, and remove all apprehension of disunion. For these objects I would not only surrender my own ease and comfort, but cheerfully lay down my life." His hopes were vain. The bombardment of Fort Sumter began on April 12, 1861, less than six weeks after his administration came to an end.

ANDREW JOHNSON
1808–1875, PRESIDENT, 1865–1869

No other "accidental President" has ever fallen heir to heavier burdens than those which descended upon the shoulders of Andrew Johnson. A Unionist from Tennessee and a Democrat, he had been nominated for Vice-President on the ticket with Lincoln in the hope that together they might secure the co-operation of the Democrats with the Republicans. He made heroic efforts to carry out the temperate reconstruction measures advocated by Lincoln, but was constantly obstructed by extremists like Charles Sumner, Thad Stevens, and Edwin Stanton. He was finally impeached by the House of Representatives and brought to trial before the Senate where he was acquitted by the narrow margin of one vote.

ULYSSES SIMPSON GRANT
1822–1885, PRESIDENT, 1869–1877

The eighteenth President was dragged into politics in spite of himself. His prominence as a soldier made him a logical candidate, but his political affiliations were so vaguely defined that for a while it seemed a toss-up as to whether the Democrats or the Republicans would nominate him. He was more in sympathy with the Republicans, however, and was twice overwhelmingly elected to the office on their platform, the second time against no less person than Horace Greeley. Grant's administration was smirched by scandal towards which his only contribution was too great trust in friends who betrayed him. It is as a soldier rather than a President that he ranks with the world's greatest.

440

JAMES ABRAM GARFIELD

1831–1881, PRESIDENT, 1881

A self-made statesman, born in a log cabin in Cuyahoga County, Ohio, Garfield had an honorable record behind him when he came to the Presidency. His service in the Civil War had been rewarded with the title of Major-General and his career in the House of Representatives had made him undisputed leader of the Republican party there. His sound qualities promised well for his administration, but on July 2, a few months after his inauguration, he was shot by a half-crazed disappointed office seeker, Charles Guiteau, and died on Sept. 19. His son, Harry Augustus, became president of Williams College from which his father was graduated in 1856.

RUTHERFORD BIRCHARD HAYES

1822–1893, PRESIDENT, 1877–1881

The Greenback party made its entrance into national politics in the Presidential campaign of 1876, but the real issue lay between the Republicans with Rutherford B. Hayes of Ohio and the Democrats with Samuel J. Tilden of New York. The contest was close. Tilden had a somewhat larger popular vote but Hayes had a majority of one in the electoral college. Both parties charged fraud and the choice was finally submitted to a special Electoral Commission of eight Republicans and seven Democrats who sustained Hayes. Mrs. Hayes was the first college graduate to become the wife of a President. She was keenly interested in public affairs and may be set down as the first modern woman in the White House.

441

CHESTER ALAN ARTHUR

1830–1886, PRESIDENT, 1881–1885

It is perhaps not fair to dismiss Chester Alan Arthur as a "machine politician of New York," but he was not a man of Presidential stature. For twenty years a successful lawyer, deeply involved in the local partisan activities of the Republican party, he was in 1871 appointed collector of the port of New York. The customs service, operating under the "spoils system," was shot through with corruption and Arthur was removed from office in 1877. He maintained that the abuses were inherent in the system, and while at first he defended the system, it is worth adding that as President he signed the Pendleton Act of 1883 which provided for competitive examinations as the basis for promotion in the Civil Service.

[STEPHEN] GROVER CLEVELAND

1837–1908, PRESIDENT, 1885–1889, 1893–1897

Grover Cleveland was the first Democrat in twenty-three years to become Chief Executive. From 1861 to his inauguration, six successive Republicans had held the office of President. He was the first President to marry in the White House and he is the only President who has served two non-consecutive terms. Benjamin Harrison, a Republican, came between his two administrations. Cleveland's second term was made especially difficult by labor troubles, financial disturbances, and a threat of war with Great Britain over a Venezuela boundary dispute, but he conducted himself with such fairness and independence that he won the respect even of his political enemies.

442

WILLIAM McKINLEY

1843–1901, PRESIDENT, 1897–1901

Even if he had never become President, McKinley would be remembered by the protective tariff bill which bears his name. After seven terms in Congress and two terms as Governor of Ohio, he was nominated for the Presidency by the Republican party. Like Harding, he conducted his campaign from his front porch and won the election, chiefly by upholding the gold standard against the free coinage of silver advocated by the Democratic candidate, William Jennings Bryan. In 1900 approval was given his conduct of the Spanish-American War when he was renominated by acclamation. The following year on Sept. 6 at the Pan-American Exposition in Buffalo he was shot by an anarchist, Leon Czolgosz, and died on Sept. 14.

BENJAMIN HARRISON

1833–1901, PRESIDENT, 1889–1893

Benjamin Harrison was the grandson of the ninth President, William Henry Harrison, and the great-grandson and namesake of the Benjamin Harrison who signed the Declaration of Independence. He had fought with conspicuous gallantry in the Civil War and had settled down to law practice in Indianapolis when he was drafted for public service. By 1888 he was Indiana's "favorite son." Pitted against Cleveland, he won the election, chiefly on the issue of protective tariff. His administration was undistinguished. The surplus in the national treasury was so large that Congress took occasion to enact various costly bills, notably the Dependent Pension Bill of 1890 which nearly doubled the government outlay for this purpose.

443

THEODORE ROOSEVELT

1858–1919, PRESIDENT, 1901–1909

One of the most versatile of the Presidents was the young New Yorker who followed McKinley. Statesman, man of letters, sportsman, naturalist, and explorer, Theodore Roosevelt began his public career at the age of twenty-three when he was elected to the New York legislature, effectively silencing his friends who warned him that politics was a "dirty business" by reminding them that the politicians were the governing class. Inaugurated at the age of forty-three, he was the youngest man ever to become President. Because of his glamorous personality, his energy, his talents, and his natural gifts as a leader of men, he is remembered as one of the most vivid as well as one of the most able of all the White House incumbents.

WILLIAM HOWARD TAFT

1857–1930, PRESIDENT, 1909–1913

When Theodore Roosevelt retired from the Presidency in 1909 he selected his Secretary of War as his successor. The Republican party acquiesced and Taft won the election by a plurality of more than a million popular votes over the Democratic nominee, William Jennings Bryan, who went down to defeat for the third and last time. Taft had not sought the office. By nature and training he was a judge, not an executive, and his ambition pointed to the Supreme Court, not the White House. This ambition was gratified in 1921 when Harding appointed him Chief Justice. He was the only man who has been both President and Chief Justice.

444

WARREN GAMALIEL HARDING

1865-1923, PRESIDENT, 1921-1923

With Wilson at the lowest ebb of his popularity, the country repudiated him and his party in the election of 1920 by giving the Republican candidate, Warren G. Harding, a majority of 7,000,000 votes over his Democratic opponent, James M. Cox. In his first message to Congress Harding begged for a "return to normalcy." He made earnest efforts in this direction, but his too great confidence in certain unworthy friends whom he made Cabinet officials has caused his administration to be remembered chiefly for the scandals connected with the Teapot Dome oil leases. He died suddenly on August 2, 1923, on the way home from Alaska, before the full import of the scandals became public.

445

[THOMAS] WOODROW WILSON

1856-1924, PRESIDENT, 1913-1921

The twenty-eighth President was fifty-five years old and nationally known as an educator when he forsook his scholarly career to become Governor of New Jersey. Two years later the split in the Republican party which followed the quarrel between Taft and Roosevelt made him President. In 1916 he was re-elected because "he kept us out of war"; our inevitable entrance into the conflict came shortly after his second inauguration. His celebrated "fourteen points" formed the basis of the peace treaty and he is regarded as the principal founder of the League of Nations. In 1920 he received the Nobel Peace Prize, his chief critic, Theodore Roosevelt, who received it in 1906 being the only other President so honored.

CALVIN COOLIDGE

1872–1933, PRESIDENT, 1923–1929

At two o'clock in the morning of August 3, 1923, when word was received from San Francisco that President Harding had died, Vice-President Coolidge succeeded to the Presidency. The oath of office was administered in the parlor of his father's farmhouse at Plymouth, Vermont, by his father, a local Justice of the Peace. His administration covered the boom years, but his watchfulness over the public treasury made "Coolidge economy" a by-word. He was reëlected in 1924 and might have been the Republican candidate for another term if he had not killed the "draft Coolidge" movement by his famous statement from the Black Hills, "I do not choose to run for President in 1928."

HERBERT CLARK HOOVER

1874–   , PRESIDENT, 1929–1933

The thirty-first President of the United States was the first Quaker and the first mining engineer to become Chief Executive. He was born in West Branch, Iowa, but his profession had carried him all over the world and his relief work in Belgium during the World War had made him an honorary citizen of that country. His only previous political experience had been gained as Secretary of Commerce, an office to which he was appointed by President Harding in 1921. The depression brought about his defeat in 1932, but his words are still potent in the councils of his party and there are few subjects today which wake more lively interest than speculations upon the probable future course of our only living ex-President.

446

FRANKLIN DELANO ROOSEVELT

1882–   , PRESIDENT, 1933

In 1921 when he was stricken with infantile paralysis at his summer home in New Brunswick, it was believed that the political career of Franklin D. Roosevelt had come to an end, but three years later he came back into the arena in support of Alfred E. Smith whom he nominated for President at the Democratic conventions of 1924 and 1928, the second time with the famous "happy warrior" speech. In the latter year he was elected Governor of New York and again in 1930. In 1933 he became President and the New Deal began. With his "fireside talks" over the radio, he has perfected a technique in governing which promises to be a powerful factor in all future national elections and administrations.